Annual Index 2014

Series Editor: Cara Acred

Complete A-Z index listings for all
ISSUES titles currently in print

Independence Educational Publishers

First published by Independence Educational Publishers

The Studio, High Green

Great Shelford

Cambridge CB22 5EG

England

British Library Cataloguing in Publication Data

Issues annual index 2014.
1. Issues--Indexes. 2. Social problems--Indexes.
I. Acred, Cara editor.
016.3'61-dc23

ISBN-13: 9781861686954

Printed in Great Britain

MWL Print Group Ltd

Vol. numbers appear first (in bold) followed by page numbers; a change in volume is preceded by a semi-colon. You can also find this title list at the back of the book.

Vol. 177 Crime in the UK
Vol. 196 Censorship Issues
Vol. 200 Sustainable Transport
Vol. 201 Mental Wellbeing
Vol. 203 The Gambling Problem
Vol. 204 The Energy Crisis
Vol. 206 Coping with Stress
Vol. 207 Consumerism and Ethics
Vol. 208 Genetic Modification
Vol. 209 Education and Society
Vol. 210 The Media
Vol. 211 Biotechnology and Cloning
Vol. 212 International Terrorism
Vol. 213 The Armed Forces
Vol. 214 Vegetarian Diets
Vol. 215 Religion in Society
Vol. 216 Tackling Climate Change
Vol. 217 Euthanasia and Assisted Suicide
Vol. 218 A Sustainable Future
Vol. 219 Class and Social Mobility
Vol. 220 Population Growth and Migration
Vol. 221 Equality and Gender Roles
Vol. 222 Tourism and Travel
Vol. 223 Crime. Punishment and Justice

Vol. 224 Domestic and Relationship Abuse
Vol. 225 LGBT Equality
Vol. 226 Globalisation and Trade
Vol. 227 Ethics in Business
Vol. 228 Illegal Drug Use
Vol. 229 Protecting Human Rights
Vol. 230 Evolution of the Internet
Vol. 231 The Abortion Debate
Vol. 232 Bullying in our Society
Vol. 233 Exploring Animal Rights
Vol. 234 Skin Deep - debating body image
Vol. 235 The Poverty Crisis
Vol. 236 Racial Discrimination
Vol. 237 Discussing Sexual Health
Vol. 238 Sexualising Society
Vol. 239 Ageing and the Elderly
Vol. 240 Citizenship in the UK
Vol. 241 Understanding Fitness
Vol. 242 Global Waste
Vol. 243 Understanding AIDS & HIV
Vol. 244 Marriage and Partnership
Vol. 245 Privacy in the UK
Vol. 246 The Sex Trade
Vol. 247 Fertility and Reproduction

Vol. 248 Discussing Child Abuse
Vol. 249 Eating Disorders
Vol. 250 Understanding Finance
Vol. 251 National Health Issues
Vol. 252 Adolescent Health
Vol. 253 The Housing Crisis
Vol.254 Understanding Alcohol
Vol.255 Disabilities
Vol.256 Cannabis
Vol.257 Families and Parenting
Vol.258 Self-harm and Suicide
Vol.259 War and Conflict
Vol.260 Endangered & Extinct Species
Vol.261 Smoking and Health
Vol.262 Homelessness in the UK
Vol.263 Careers and Unemployment
Vol.264 Student Choices
Vol.265 Understanding Depression
Vol.266 Social Media
Vol.267 Death and Bereavement
Vol.268 Child Labour & Exploitation
Vol.269 Alternative Healing
Vol.270 Sport in our Society
Vol.271 Food and Diet in the UK

Titles of publications are in *italics.*

12 Step programmes **203**.25
4G mobile spectrum **230**.1
40 Days for Life campaign **231**.34, 35

A&E departments
   and self-harm **258**.5
   waiting times **251**.17
A-levels (Advanced Level)
   options after A-levels **264**.1-3
   as predictor of degree performance **209**.12;
     219.32
abandoned properties **253**.34-5
Abdul-Qaadir, Bilqis (basketball player) **270**.24-5
abortion **231**.1-39
   aborted fetuses in stem cell trials **211**.33
   alternatives to **231**.8, 17-18
   anti-abortion campaigns **231**.34-5
   arguments against (pro-life) **231**.1, 16
   arguments for (pro-choice) **231**.1, 16
   counselling **231**.24-5, 26-9, 31, 36-7
   and disability **231**.20
   effects **231**.5, 6-7
     on men **231**.9
     on mental health **231**.14-15
   ethical issues **231**.16-29
   and the law **231**.1-2, 3, 32
   private clinics
     and advertising **231**.38
     and counseling **231**.24-5
     gender abortion **231**.30-31
     NHS funding **231**.24
   procedure **231**.6-7
   reasons for abortions **231**.13, 32
   religious positions on **231**.19

   risks **231**.6-7
   sex-selection abortion **231**.18, 30-31
   statistics **231**.10-12
   time limit **231**.21-3
Abortion Act 1967 **231**.1
absolute poverty **235**.1, 2-3
abuse
   adults' behaviour at children's sports matches
     270.28-9
   child abuse in sport **270**.26-7
   and children's mental health **201**.3
   class-based **219**.5-6
   of disabled people **255**.37
   elder abuse **239**.34
   racist abuse
     in football **236**.9, 12, 13, 15, 38, 39
     on Twitter **236**.31
   see also domestic abuse; emotional abuse;
neglect; physical abuse; sexual abuse abusers
   child abusers **248**.6, 26
   domestic, help for **224**.39
academic achievement *see* educational
achievement
academic learning style in schools **209**.2
academic qualifications
   versus vocational qualifications
   see also exams
Academies Programme **209**.25, 26
   and social mobility **219**.28
access to children *see* contact
Access to Work **255**.33
accidents
   alcohol-related **254**.16-17
   road accidents **200**.12
achievement *see* educational achievement
ACMD (Advisory Council on the Misuse of Drugs)
   228.25-6, 27
ACPO Child Protection Delivery Plan **248**.36
acquired immunodeficiency syndrome *see* AIDS
Action on Sugar campaign group **271**.20
active euthanasia **217**.5
activity, physical
Acts of Union **240**.32

acupuncture **269**.2, 25
    and dementia treatment **269**.21
    and depression treatment **265**.29
    health and safety **269**.9
    in palliative care **269**.23
addictions
    alcohol **254**.1-2, 8-9
        drug prescriptions **254**.10
        and minimum alcohol pricing **254**.38
    cannabis **256**.6 8, 12, 17, 23
        signs **256**.14
    Facebook **230**.15
    gambling **203**.6, 20
        see also problem gambling
    Internet **230**.14, 16-18
    nicotine **261**.3, 4-5
    pornography **246**.1-2
    shopping **207**.6
    smoking **252**.38
    social media **230**.15; **266**.13
    synthetic cannabinoids **256**.4
    see also dependency
additives *see* food additives
ADD *see* attention deficit disorder
additional paternity leave **221**.4-5
adjustment disorder related to bereavement **267**.6
administrators of an estate **267**.29
adoption **247**.14-17
    adopted children and education **247**.17
    adoption leave and pay **247**.16
    adoption process **247**.15
    as alternative to abortion **231**.8, 17-18
    contact with birth family **247**.16
    illegal, as trafficking **268**.38-9
    of obese children **241**.23
    by same-sex couples **225**.34; **257**.17-18
Adoption of Children Act 1926 **248**.35
adult learners **209**.39
adult stem cells **211**.28, 29
adultery as grounds for divorce **244**.30
advance decisions (medical treatment) **217**.13, 35-6
advance statements **217**.35
Adventist Health Study 2 **214**.31-2
advertising
    abortion clinics **231**.38
    and age **196**.20
    airbrushing and unrealistic body images **234**.24-
        6, 27-8
    and children **207**.35-6, 37, 39; **234**.23
        on social media websites **266**.24
    children's awareness of gambling advertising **203**.13
    junk food **271**.27-30
    media advertising spending **210**.15
    online **230**.5
    and pressure to spend **250**.32
    regulation and body confidence issues **234**.21
    sexual services **246**.23
    and sexualized imagery **238**.5, 6-7
    tobacco, and children, Indonesia **261**.39
    see also marketing
Advisory Council on the Misuse of Drugs (ACMD)
    228.25-6, 27
aerobic activity **241**.25

aesthetic surgery *see* cosmetic surgery
affluence *see* wealth
affordable home ownership schemes **253**.6, 7-8, 9
affordable housing construction **253**.28
Afghanistan conflict **259**.1, 32-3
    after death of Osama bin Laden **212**.24-5
    impact on women's rights **259**.34
Africa
    AIDS strategy support **243**.29
    armed conflicts **259**.2
        child casualties **259**.25
    child labour **268**.11
    child malnutrition **259**.26
    child soldiers **259**.24
    criminalization of homosexuality **225**.39
    elephant and rhino poaching **260**.9-11, 23, 24-5
    gender inequality **221**.1
    HIV/AIDS infection rates **243**.26, 27
        older people with HIV **243**.20
    hunting and conservation **260**.30-31
    internally displaced people **259**.18
    poverty rates **235**.23, 24
    and Prince William **260**.8-9
African Charter on the Rights and Welfare of the
Child **268**.25
African communities, attitudes to HIV/AIDS **243**.16-17
African people and HIV risk **243**.8
age
    and advertising **196**.20
    and cannabis use **256**.15-16
    and childhood aggression **224**.23
    of criminal responsibility **223**.30, 31-2
    of death, homeless people **262**.20
    in domestic violence definition **224**.35-6
    and eating disorders **249**.4
    and fertility **247**.2, 4, 5, 6
    of foetal viability **231**.21, 22
    for purchasing tobacco, New York **261**.30
    IVF and older women **247**.10, 22-5
    legal drinking age **254**.21
    of motherhood **257**.10
    of smokers **261**.6
    and social media use **266**.16
    and sport participation **270**.1, 3
    voting age lowering **240**.30-31
age discrimination **239**.4, 8, 12-13
    in home care **229**.33
    NHS ban **239**.11
    against young people **239**.6-7
age ratings
    music videos **238**.5
    video games **196**.17
age structure of population, global **220**.8
ageing **239**.1-39
    ageing experience, international comparisons **239**.8-9
    ageing process **239**.1-2
    costs of ageing population **239**.15
    and health **239**.3-4, 24-39
    lesbian, gay and bisexual people **239**.10-11
    people with HIV **243**.19-20, 30-31
    stereotypes **239**.4-5
    young peoples' attitudes to **239**.6-7
    see also older people

ageing population
    global **220**.8; **239**.3, 4, 13
    UK **239**.15, 16
ageism *see* age discrimination
Agenda 21 and waste management **242**.4
aggressive behaviour in children **224**.22-3
agoraphobia **252**.14
agriculture
    and animal welfare **233**.2, 3
    and climate change **216**.11
    environmental impact **214**.16, 17, 22-3
    factory farming **233**.3, 7-8
    fairtrade *see* fair trade
    fur farming **233**.18, 19
    mega-farms **233**.3, 9-11
    migrant workers **263**.10-11
    subsidies, impact on developing countries **226**.33
    sustainable meat production **214**.14, 20-21, 23
    waste produce harvested for charities **242**.39
    see also animal welfare; food production;
    genetically modified (GM) crops
aid
    aid for trade **226**.34
    definitions **235**.32
    and disabled people, Uganda **255**.39
    displaced people, Syria **259**.20
    effectiveness **235**.31-2
    and gay rights **225**.14
    mobile apps for aid workers **266**.34
    and slums **235**.38
    and wildlife conservation **260**.33
AIDS (Acquired Immune Deficiency Syndrome)
    AIDS-related deaths **243**.6, 26, 27
    definition **243**.1
    global targets **243**.26-7
    government health campaign (1986) **251**.2
    symptoms **243**.2-3
    timeline **243**.7
    treatments *see* antiretroviral therapy (ART)
    see also HIV (Human Immunodeficiency Virus)
air pollution *see* emissions
air source heat pumps **204**.35
air travel
    air passenger duty tax **222**.14-15
    emissions from **200**.14, 24
    environmental impact **200**.24-5
airbrushing and body image **234**.5, 18, 24-6, 27-8
aircraft carriers and defence budget cuts **213**.21
al-Qaida
    and Afghanistan conflict **212**.24-5
    after death of Osama bin Laden **212**.23
    terrorist attacks in Great Britain **212**.6
Alabaré Home for Veterans **262**.33
alcohol **254**.1-39
    beer industry **254**.39
    binge drinking *see* binge drinking
    and brain impairment **201**.10; **254**.3, 5
    consumption
        after divorce **244**.32
        cutting down **254**.7, 17; **271**.25
        elderly people **239**.33
        global guidelines **254**.18
        UK consumption falling **254**.25
        under-reporting **254**.23-4

    young people **252**.2, 31, 35; **254**.26, 27, 28
    counterfeit (fake) alcohol **254**.13, 38
    dependence **254**.1-2, 8-9
        drug prescriptions **254**.10
        and minimum alcohol pricing **254**.38
    and depression **265**.3
    and domestic violence **224**.6
    drinking behaviour
        binge drinking **254**.2, 4, 23-4
        problem drinking **254**.1-2, 8-9
        young people **254**.26, 28, 29-31, 32
    effects of **254**.1, 3-4, 16
        on appearance **254**.3
    and elderly people **239**.33
    health risks **254**.1, 3-4, 5-6, 7, 8
        from fake alcohol **254**.13
    inhaling alcohol **254**.33-4
    and the law
        legal drinking age **254**.21
        see also drink-driving
    mental health effects **254**.1, 3, 5, 6
    minimum unit pricing **254**.14, 19, 37-8
    retailers' Code of Practice **254**.22
    and sex **237**.3
    and stress **206**.33
    and students **254**.35-6
        see also young people and alcohol
    units of **254**.2, 11-12
        and physical and mental effects **254**.7
    see also binge drinking; young people and
alcohol
alcohol abuse
    and homeless people stereotyping **262**.14
    and mental illness **201**.17
        see also dual diagnosis
    see also alcohol, dependence; underage drinking
alcohol-related accidents **254**.16-17
alcohol-related hospital admissions **254**.14
alcohol strategy consultation, government response
    254.19-20
alcohol without liquid (AWOL) **254**.33-4
algae biofuels **204**.34
aloe vera **269**.26-7
alternative therapies **269**.1-39
    and cancer **269**.6, 7, 19
    choosing a practitioner **269**.8-9, 11, 21, 23
    definition **269**.8
    future of **269**.5-6
    types **269**.1-4
    see also acupuncture; herbal medicines;
homeopathy
alternative tourism **222**.16
    definition **222**.24
    see also ecotourism; voluntourism
Alternative Vote (AV) **240**.29
Alzheimer's disease **239**.24, 28
    and animal research **233**.36
Alzheimer's Society **201**.11
Americas, press freedom **196**.2
Amnesty International
    and armed conflict **259**.2
    campaigns on human rights and children **268**.14
    response to UK counter-terrorism review **212**.38-9
Amy Winehouse Foundation **228**.10-11

anabolic steroids **228**.26; **270**.30-31
anaerobic digestion plant for food waste **242**.38
anal sex **237**.4
Andaz Liverpool Street hotel, employing homeless people **262**.39
Anderson, William **265**.30
anger and grief **267**.2, 8
anger management **206**.3
angina **239**.24
Anglican Church and abortion **231**.19
animal cloning **211**.7-21
    Dolly the sheep **211**.7, 8
    ethical concerns **211**.10-11
    for food production **211**.6, 10-19
Animal Defenders International **233**.4
animal experimentation **233**.3, 28-39
    alternatives to **233**.28, 32
    and animal welfare societies **233**.1
    arguments against **233**.35-6
    arguments for **233**.37-8
    and genetically modified animals **211**.37-8
    myths and facts **233**.30-33
    reasons for **233**.28
    regulation of **233**.28, 33
    types of animals used **233**.29, 33
animal feed, GM content **208**.8, 24
animal fights **233**.6, 17, 27
animal rights
    whales and dolphins **233**.20-21
    see also animal welfare
animal welfare **233**.1-6
    circuses **233**.14-15
    and cloning **211**.10, 19
    and farming **233**.7-11
    and fur trade **233**.3-4, 18-19
    UK legislation on **233**.1-2, 5-6
    and vegetarianism **214**.5
Animal Welfare Act **233**.2, 5-6
    and film classification **196**.14
animals
    genetic modification *see* genetically modified animals
    homosexual behaviour **225**.15
    see also pets
annualised hours **263**.33
anorexia athletica **249**.7
anorexia nervosa **249**.1, 6
    causes **249**.32
    causing death of model **234**.36
    effects **249**.32, 35
    force feeding of patient **249**.38-9
    mealtime support **249**.37
    treatment **249**.33
Antarctic ice sheet and climate change **216**.12
anti-abortion campaigns **231**.34-5
antibiotics
    resistance to **269**.6
    use in farming **233**.7
anti-bullying policies
    schools **232**.18
    and sexuality **232**.15
anti-bullying strategies **232**.3-4, 16, 19-21
    cyberbullying **232**.26-7, 28, 29, 39

schools **232**.3, 10, 18
anticipated stigma about HIV **243**.16-17
antidepressant drugs **206**.3; **265**.4, 19-22
    and anxiety **206**.13
    for children and young people **252**.19
    and grief **267**.4
    and postnatal depression **265**.13
    and seasonal affective disorder **265**.11
    side effects **265**.20, 21
    and suicide **258**.27; **265**.21-2
anti-Muslim   hate crime **215**.28-30; **236**.14, 24
    see also Islamophobia
anti-pornography campaign **246**.6
anti-racism laws *see* legislation and racism
antiretroviral therapy (ART) **243**.3-4
    curing baby born with HIV **243**.37-9
    worldwide access to **243**.6
anti-Semitism **215**.36
    football chants **236**.39
Anti-Social Behaviour, Crime and Policing bill, and homelessness **262**.18
anti-social behaviour orders
    and children **268**.17
    and prostitution **246**.21, 25
anti-terrorism *see* counter-terrorism
Anti-terrorism Crime and Security Act 2001 **212**.19
anxiety **206**.10-15; **252**.13-15
    causes **206**.11-12
    definition **206**.10, 14
    managing **265**.3
    medication **206**.13
    symptoms of **206**.10-11; **265**.17
appearance
    effects of alcohol **254**.3
    effects of smoking **261**.8-9, 25
apprenticeships **209**.38; **264**.2, 3, 6, 8
    compared with university **264**.9
    gender segregation **221**.28
    higher **264**.2, 3, 6
approved mental health professionals **201**.38
aptitude tests for university admission **219**.32
Arab Spring
    and human rights violations **229**.9
    and social media **266**.28
architecture of the home and privacy **245**.2
armed conflict *see* war
Armed Forces **213**.1-39
    accomodation for veterans **262**.33
    Armed Forces Covenant **213**.25-7, 28
    Army life **213**.1-2
    deaths **213**.9
    ex-service personnel *see* ex-service personnel
    injured personnel **213**.7, 8-9, 10-11
    and mental health **213**.3-6
    post traumatic stress disorder **213**.3-4, 5, 34
    and sexual orientation, USA **225**.38-9
    Strategic Defence and Security Review **213**.17-21
    suicides **258**.31
    Territorial Army **213**.30
    under-18s recruitment **268**.27
    and women **213**.12-14
    and young people **213**.15-16
arms embargoes **259**.10
Arms Trade Treaty **259**.16-17

aromatherapy **269**.3-4
    and dementia treatment **269**.21
    and palliative care **269**.23
arranged marriages **244**.12
arrests of British nationals overseas **222**.15
Article 8, Human Rights Act **245**.1
ASBOs *see* anti-social behaviour orders
ASD (autistic specturm disorders) **255**.3, 6-8
Asia
    criminalization of homosexuality **225**.39
    poverty rates **235**.23, 24, 25
Asia-Pacific region
    internally displaced people **259**.18
    press freedom **196**.2
Asian people, British identity **240**.6
Asperger sundrome **255**.3, 6
Aspinall, Damian **260**.32
Assange, Julian (WikiLeaks) **210**.20-21
assaults on school staff **209**.16
assistance dogs **255**.18-19
assisted dying
    arguments for **217**.38-9
    legislation **217**.2
    see also assisted suicide; euthanasia
Assisted Dying for the Terminally Ill bill **217**.2
assisted reproductive technologies (ART) *see* fertility treatments
assisted suicide **217**.5
    arguments against **217**.3-4
    arguments for **217**.3
    cases **217**.20, 21
    doctors' opposition to **217**.22
    physician-assisted suicide **217**.22, 24-5
    prevalence in UK **217**.24-5
    public attitudes to **217**.23, 34
    see also assisted dying; euthanasia
asthma **252**.7
astro-tourism **222**.17-18
asylum seekers **259**.23
    children **268**.18
    young,and mental health problems **201**.2
atheists, protesting against religious faith **196**.11-12
athletes
    attributes of success **270**.10-11
    and drugs *see* drugs in sport
    and eating disorders **249**.16
    foreign born athletes in British Olympic team **240**.10-11
    psychological effects of injury **270**.37-8
    school and community visits **270**.7
    transsexual **270**.18-19
    working conditions **270**.8-9
Australia
    cannabis laws **256**.29
    health care **251**.9
    Internet censorship **196**.30
    transgender rights **225**.24
autistic spectrum disorders (ASD) **255**.3, 6-8
aversion therapy for homosexual behaviour **225**.16
aviation *see* air travel
Avon Foundation **227**.21
AWOL (alcohol without liquid) **254**.33-4

B

babies
    born with HIV **243**.1-2, 26-7
        cured of HIV **243**.37-9
        life as teenagers **243**.23-5
    neonatal death **267**.22
    physical activity guidelines **241**.6
    premature, viability **231**.21, 22
    stillbirth **267**.21-2
Baby P **248**.1
Bachman, Melissa **260**.29
back pain and acupuncture **269**.2
badger cull **260**.22
bail, in Legal Aid, Sentencing and Punishment of Offenders Bill **223**.25
Bailey Review on sexualisation of childhood **238**.2, 5-7, 8, 33, 34
balanced diet *see* healthy eating
Bamu, Kristy **248**.22
banana trade **226**.35
Bangkok climate change negotiations **216**.37
Bangladesh, girls' education **244**.15
banks
    bail-outs **227**.16
    customer attitudes **250**.7, 8
    taxation **235**.13-15
    use of tax havens **227**.36
Barber, Brendan, on unemployment **263**.3
Barbie body image **234**.31
Barnado's report on child sex trafficking **246**.35-6
bariatric (weight loss) surgery
    cost effectiveness **241**.18
    for teenagers **241**.22
barristers, ethnic minorities **236**.12
basketball, ban on wearing hijab **270**.24
bats, endangered **260**.1, 7
battery farmed chickens **233**.3, 7
BBC
    Choosing to Die documentary **217**.20
    Editorial Guidelines **210**.27
    Ofcom regulation **196**.20
    radio and TV services **210**.3
BDD *see* body dysmorphic disorder
beauty pageants for children **238**.28-30
bed and breakfast hotels, homeless families **262**.11
Beddington, John, and homeopathy debate **269**.32, 34, 35
beer industry **254**.39
behaviour
    effects of sexual abuse **248**.4, 26
    pupils, and teacher stress **209**.15
    signs of drug use **228**.15
    stress and behavioural changes **206**.19
Belgium, euthanasia **217**.2, 32
beliefs
    and death **267**.23
    see also humanism; religion
benefits *see* state benefits
Benefits Street (Channel 4) **263**.12
benign ignorance (indirect racism) **236**.28
bereavement
    children **201**.2
    complicated (prolonged) **267**.3-4, 6-7

funerals *see* funerals
grieving **267**.1-4, 6-7
losing a pet **267**.8-10
mourning clothes **267**.12
practical matters **267**.28-30
remembering *see* remembrance of the deceased
support **267**.3
see also death
Bergen Facebook Addiction Scale **230**.15
Berlin Patient **243**.32, 33
Bern Convention **260**.27
betel quid (chewing tobacco) **261**.10
betting **203**.4
see also gambling
Bevan, Aneurin **219**.12
Bhagavad Gita and war and peace **259**.3
big cats
endangered **260**.6, 36-7
lion hunting **260**.29, 30-31
see also tigers
Big Issue **262**.17
Big Society **240**.33-4
bigamy **244**.3
bigorexia **249**.7
bikes *see* cycling
Bill Gates Foundation **259**.29
bin Laden, Osama, effect of death on al-Qaida
212.23
binge drinking **254**.2, 4, 23-4
young people **252**.36
binge eating disorder **249**.2, 6-7
bingo **203**.4
bins, homeless people dying in **262**.21
biodegradable products, environmental impact **218**.37
biodiesel, from algae **204**.34
biodiversity
conservation, marine environments **218**.22-3
and ecotourism **222**.28
loss **218**.14, 18
public attitudes to **216**.11; **218**.17
and tourism **222**.22-3, 28
bioenergy *see* biomass energy
bio-fortification **208**.19
biofuels **204**.3, 26, 32, 39; **208**.22
from algae **204**.34
biological causes of criminal behaviour **223**.11
biomarker for depression **265**.14
biomass energy **204**.3, 6, 26
Drax power plant **204**.5, 7
biomaterials **208**.21
biometrics **245**.33
biotechnology
applications **211**.4
definition **211**.1, 4
history **211**.2-3
see also cloning; genetic modification
bipolar affective disorder (manic depression)
201.14-15, 24-5; **265**.1-2
experiences of sufferers **201**.14-15; **265**.9-10
bird populations, UK **260**.21-2
birth control *see* contraception
birth rates
and abortion rate, UK **231**.11
global **220**.2, 4, 9, 13, 15

and marital status **257**.3, 10
UK **257**.10
see also teenage pregnancies
birth registration and children's rights **268**.20
bisexuality *see* LGBT people
Black Dog Tribe **266**.27
black people
students, employment prospects **236**.19-20
women and poverty **221**.34
young people and mental health problems **201**.2
see also employment and racism; ethnic
minorities; racism
Black Report on health care **251**.2
bladder, effects of alcohol **254**.3
blast mines **259**.9
blended families **257**.22-3
blessing ceremonies
civil partnerships **244**.17
marriages **244**.3
blogging **210**.16; **266**.1
blood donation, from gay and bisexual men **225**.36-7
blood doping risks **270**.31
blood pressure
effect of marijuana **256**.8
effect of salt intake **271**.12
high blood pressure **241**.4
blood products and HIV **243**.1
blood sugar and mental health **252**.25
blood tests for HIV diagnosis **243**.3
BMA and abortion counselling **231**.28, 29
BMI *see* body mass index
BNP *see* British National Party
boardroom positions
gender quotas **221**.16, 21
women **221**.14, 15, 16, 17-18, 20, 21-2, 37
body confidence promotion
Girlguiding UK **234**.34
government campaign **234**.20-21, 37, 39
parent pack **234**.39
in schools **234**.11, 21, 29-30
body dysmorphic disorder/dysmorphophobia **249**.7
body image **234**.1-39
Barbie ideal **234**.31
and fashion industry **234**.5-6, 11
improving **234**.1-3
and the media **234**.5, 7, 8, 10, 11, 18
men **234**.13, 16-17
negative **234**.1
and pornography **246**.1
positive *see* body confidence promotion
and young people **234**.7, 26
body mass index (BMI) **241**.14, 17; **249**.5; **271**.
14-15
and meat-eating **214**.35
body talk
men **234**.16-17
women **234**.8
body weight
effects of alcohol **254**.6
and fertility **247**.3, 5
see also obesity; weight management
Bolivia, education programme **229**.28
bones, effects of alcohol **254**.6
Bonn Convention **260**.27

bonuses
  and inequality **227**.15
  justification of **227**.19
bookmarking services (social media) **266**.1-2
books, self-help, depression **265**.31
Born and Red families **257**.8
Bornean orangutan **260**.26
borrowing *see* debt
bottom billion **235**.28-9
BoxeR (video gamer) **270**.34
boys and young men
  biomarker for depression **265**.14
  and eating disorders **249**.17-19
  and education
    attitude to school **209**.11
    single-sex schools **221**.30
  gender stereotyping in boys' clothing **238**.1
  and parental separation **244**.36
  and sexual violence **238**.17
  stereotype pressures **238**.3
  talking about problems **265**.28
  teenage dads, need for support **257**.34
  toy preferences **221**.7-8
brain
  effects of ageing **239**.2
  effects of alcohol **201**.10; **254**.3, 5
  effects of cannabis **256**.2, 8, 22-4
  effects of smoking **261**.4, 5
  and sexual orientation **225**.15-16
brain damage and gambling **203**.7
brain drain **220**.32-3
brands
  national versus store brands **207**.11
  ownership of ethical brands **207**.31
  tobacco marketing and children **261**.33
Brazil
  censorship of sexual content on the Internet **196**.37
  economic development **226**.20-21
  privacy rights **245**.4
  wellbeing of older people **239**.9
Break the Bag Habit campaign **242**.25
breakfast
  children going without **271**.4
  healthy eating choices **271**.31, 32
Breaking the Cycle Green Paper **223**.23
breast cancer as cause of death **267**.20
breast screening programme **251**.2
Breath of Addiction (film) **261**.15
bribery and corruption in business **227**.31
bricks and walls layer of privacy **245**.2
bright light therapy and dementia treatment **269**.21
Brighton Housing Trust, shipping containers as
accommodation **262**.31
BringBackOurGirls campaign **266**.38
Britain *see* UK
British Board of Film Classification (BBFC) **196**.13-16
  and legislation **196**.14
British Crime Survey **223**.3-5
British Heart Foundation and animal research
  233.36
British identity **240**.6, 8, 12-14
  ethnic minorities **240**.18-20
  Muslims **240**.17-18
  and national origins **240**.15-16

and social group **240**.20
and the Union Jack **240**.4-5
Youth Parliament manifesto **240**.39
British Medical Association (BMA) and abortion
counselling **231**.28, 29
British National Party **236**.37
  inclusion in political debates **196**.7, 8
British people, emotional behaviour **267**.4-5
British tourists
  arrested or hospitalised overseas **222**.15
  holidaying at home **222**.5
Britishness *see* British identity
broadband services **230**.6-8
  super-fast broadband **210**.15
broadcasters
  freedom of expression **196**.24
  regulation **196**.18-20; **210**.27
  see also radio; television
Brook **237**.36
brothels
  and the law **246**.21-2
  legalization **246**.26
Brown, Louise **247**.13
Brown, Timothy Ray (Berlin Patient) **243**.32, 33
Buddhism **215**.1
  and abortion **231**.19
  non-violence **259**.3-4
  and vegetarianism **214**.6
budgeting
  and debt repayment **250**.37-8
  students **264**.19
Bulger, James **248**.35
bulimia nervosa **249**.1-2, 6, 18-19
  Amy Winehouse **249**.24
  diabetes sufferers **249**.11
  treatment **249**.33
bullfighting **233**.17
bullies
  characteristics of **232**.2
  consequences for **232**.22
bullying **232**.1-39
  children with gender-variant behaviour **225**.24
  cyber-bullying *see* cyberbullying
  dealing with bullying **232**.3, 17, 18, 19-21
    cyberbullying **232**.3, 26, 29, 39
    in the workplace **232**.23, 24
  of disabled people **255**.37
  and eating disorders **249**.21
  effects **232**.3, 8, 21, 22
    of cyberbullying **232**.25, 26
    on mental health **201**.2
  forms of bullying behaviour **232**.1, 21-2
  homophobic **225**.8, 9, 29; **232**.12-13, 15
  laws concerning **225**.7
    cyberbullying **232**.34-5, 37
  LGBT pupils **225**.8
  by mobile phone **232**.17, 25, 27, 29
  prevalence of **232**.30, 31
  punishment for **232**.22
  racist **232**.10, 11, 17; **236**.16
  reasons for **232**.2, 14, 25-6
  reporting **232**.20
    cyberbullying **232**.29, 36, 39
    workplace **232**.24

sexual **221**.11
signs of **232**.2-3
and social media **227**.38; **232**.25, 26-7, 28
statistics **232**.4
in student halls **264**.31
and suicide **232**.9
victims **232**.2, 8
at work *see* workplace bullying
see also bullies; school bullying; workplace
bullying
burial
costs **267**.34
green burials **267**.36
of a pet **267**.9
burnout (overwork) **263**.32, 36
burqa wearing
arguments for and against **215**.37-8
prohibition in European countries **215**.34-6
public opinions **215**.39
bursaries, students **250**.24
buses
bus lane on M4 **200**.36
electric **200**.28-9
guided busways **200**.30, 32
straddling bus **200**.29
usage **200**.3
business ownership aspirations **227**.6
businesses **227**.1-39
and child labour elimination **268**.12
corporate responsibility **227**.9-30
and economic growth **227**.14
employing young people **263**.26-7
new working practices **227**.1-3
partnerships with universities **264**.6
public attitudes to **227**.13-14
start-ups **227**.5
by young people **264**.10-11
statistics **227**.4-5, 6
and tax **227**.32-6
butterfly numbers **260**.21
buying a home
Help to Buy schemes **253**.6, 7-8, 9, 25
pros and cons **253**.6
young people's difficulties **253**.2-3, 5
see also home ownership

C

Cabinet, The **240**.26
Cadbury, accused of racist advertising **236**.29
caffeine drinks **271**.10, 24
calcium-rich foods **271**.23-4
California, cannabis policy **256**.31-2
CALM (Campaign Against Living Miserably) **252**.15
calorie content of alcohol **254**.6
calorie intake **271**.23
Victorian diet **271**.1
CAM *see* complementary and alternative medicine
CAMbrella, research into complementary medicine **269**.10
camera development and privacy law **245**.2-3
Cameron, David

on economic policy **263**.3
entrepreneurship campaign **227**.7
on immigration policy **220**.30-31
on nuclear weapons **259**.15
Campaign Against Living Miserably (CALM) **252**.15
campaigning and social media **266**.38
charity campaigns **266**.35, 36
Campbell, Naomi, accusing Cadbury of racism **236**.29
camping holidays, luxury **222**.20
Canada
AIDS strategy support **243**.28
cannabis laws **256**.29
as gap year destination **222**.19
health care **251**.9
seal hunting **233**.22, 23
cancer **239**.24
and alcohol consumption **254**.5
and cannabis use **228**.9; **256**.8, 21
as cause of death **267**.20
children and young people **252**.7-8
complementary and alternative therapies **269**.6-9, 19, 28-30
dangers **269**.31
conventional treatment **269**.7-8
and physical activity **241**.2
and red meat consumption **214**.35
and smoking **261**.1, 8
and vegetarian diets **214**.38-9
see also cervical cancer; lung cancer; cancer
awareness campaigns; and social media **266**.35, 36
Cancer Research UK, funding animal research **233**.35, 38
Cancun Agreement **226**.4
Cancun climate change conference **216**.37, 39
cannabinoids **256**.2
synthetic **256**.3-4
cannabis **256**.1-39
chemical make-up **256**.2
classification **256**.1, 27
cultivation
campaign to help public recognise cannabis
farms **256**.39
sentencing guidelines **228**.30-31
dependence on **256**.6, 8, 12, 17, 23
signs **256**.14
user characteristics **256**.15-16
effects of **228**.14; **256**.2, 11-26
on the brain **256**.2, 8, 22-4
cancer healing claims **228**.9
on education and learning **256**.11
forms of **256**.1
giving up **256**.13
and hard drug use **256**.8, 34, 37
health risks **256**.8, 9, 11-13, 17, 21, 32; **270**.32
history **256**.7
and the law **256**.1-2, 27-39
legalisation debate **256**.30-38
medicinal use of **256**.19, 20, 29
and mental health **228**.8; **256**.11-12, 20, 32, 34, 35-6
penalties
for possession **256**.2, 27-9
sentencing guidelines **228**.28-9, 30-31
for supply **256**.27
production *see* cannabis cultivation

psychosis **256**.12
reasons for using **256**.5-6
reclassification **256**.1, 27
and schizophrenia **228**.8; **256**.11-12, 34, 35-6
signs of use **228**.14
taxing the cannabis market **256**.10
usage statistics **256**.17, 30
capitalism, defence of **227**.17, 18-19
car-free days **200**.19-20
carbon dioxide and GM crops **208**.20, 22
carbon dioxide emissions
EU targets **204**.30
and population growth **220**.14
UK targets **204**.28-9
see also greenhouse gas
carbon footprint, GM food **208**.29
carbon offsetting **216**.35-6
and inequality **218**.3-4
and rainforest protection **218**.20-21
cardiopulmonary resuscitation (CPR) **217**.13-14
cardiovascular disease (CVD)
caused by stress **206**.4
and eating red meat **214**.35
incidence in UK **241**.2
see also heart disease
care, social *see* care services for older people;
social care
Care Quality Commission (CQC) **251**.26, 31
care services for older people
concerns of lesbian, gay and bisexual people **239**.10-
11
funding **239**.20-23
and human rights **229**.33-4
need for **239**.4
cared-for children **268**.18
going missing **248**.28
and mental health problems **201**.3-4
career aspirations and gender **221**.21, 28-9
Career Colleges **264**.7
careers guidance services **264**.4
carers **255**.21
children **255**.20-21
and financial insecurity **263**.16-17
for people with autism **255**.8
support for **255**.1
young carers and neglect **248**.15
Caribbean countries, criminalization of
homosexuality **225**.39
carnivores, large
endangered **260**.6, 36-7
see also lions; tigers
carrier bags *see* plastic bags
cars
car clubs **200**.11
congestion *see* congestion, traffic
drink-driving *see* drink-driving
electric **200**.26, 27; **204**.7
emissions reduction **200**.15
impact on health **200**.1, 23
methane-powered **204**.39
reducing use of **200**.7-8, 19-20, 25, 26
sharing **200**.25
see also driving; road accidents
cash payments **250**.3

casinos
being sued for gambler's losses **203**.38
casino games **203**.4
casual racism **236**.29-30
Catholic Church
and abortion **231**.19, 39
Catholic Relief Services **259**.29
see also Christianity
cattle
cloning **211**.12, 13-17
see also livestock farming
CBT (Convention on Biological Diversity) **260**.28
CBT *see* Cognitive Behavioural Therapy
CCTV (Closed Circuit Television) **245**.28-9
and analysis of shopper behaviour **245**.35
code of practice consultation **245**.32
concerns about **245**.31
public involvement in monitoring **245**.30
rights to see footage **245**.29
in schools **245**.36-7
celebrities
and body image **234**.6-7
and cyberbullying **232**.38
in girls' magazines **238**.13
and health advice **252**.5
libel actions **210**.38
cell ageing **239**.1
censorship
films **196**.13, 14
and the Internet **196**.27-39
sexual content on the Internet **196**.36-8
census, religious belief data **215**.5
centenarians **239**.1
Central African Republic **235**.39
Central and Eastern Europe, press freedom **196**.2
Centre for Appearance Research (CAR) **234**.4, 15
Centrepoint **262**.23, 24
Centrepoint Sleep Out campaign **262**.37
CEOP (Child Exploitation and Online Protection
Centre) **248**.35
cervical cancer **237**.28-9
and HPV **237**.26
screening **237**.27, 28, 32
vaccination **237**.26-7, 28, 29-31
cetaceans' rights **233**.20-21
CGI (Clinton Global Initiative) **260**.24-5
Chadwick, Edwin **219**.11
Chance to Shine cricket scheme **232**.7
Change4Life programme **271**.6
character skills and children's attainment **219**.34-5
charities
animal welfare **233**.1
and the Big Society **240**.34
business support for **227**.20-21
caring for wounded troops **213**.7
fraud **207**.21, 22
medical, funding animal research **233**.35-8
poverty aid **235**.32
and social media **266**.35-7
Charles, Prince of Wales
and homeopathy debate **269**.36
speech at Illegal Wildlife Trade Conference **260**.18-
20
Charter Schools, USA **209**.20

chatrooms and bullying **232**.25, 36
chavs, prejudice against **219**.5
chelation therapy **269**.4
Chemical Weapons Convention **259**.10
chemicals
    in cigarettes **261**.3
    in e-cigarettes **261**.11, 13
    pollution from pharmaceutical waste **218**.38-9
    UK exports to Syria **259**.11
chemotherapy nausea and acupuncture **269**.2
chewing and spitting (eating disorders) **249**.8
chewing tobacco **261**.10
chickens *see* hens
child abuse **248**.1-39
    effects **248**.3-5, 26
    faith-based abuse **248**.21-3
    getting help **248**.14-15, 26-7
    images on the Internet **196**.39
    and mental health problems **201**.3
    neglect **248**.3, 14-20
    physical **248**.3
    prevalence **248**.5-6, 7
    signs **248**.4, 15, 30
    in sport **270**.26-7, 28-9
    see also corporal punishment; sexual abuse
Child B case **248**.22
child exploitation **268**.31-9
    see also child labour; sexual exploitation of children
Child Exploitation and Online Protection (CEOP) Centre **248**.35
child labour **229**.15-16; **268**.1-12
    definitions **268**.1, 2
    and education **221**.39; **268**.22-3
    elimination **268**.4, 12
    prevalence **268**.2-3, 10-11
    reasons for **268**.3
    tobacco industry **261**.9, 39
Child Labour Index **268**.10-11
child maintenance **257**.30-31
child marriage **244**.15; **248**.24-5; 28-30
child-on-child abuse **238**.17; **248**.13
child pornography
    legal status, worldwide **246**.9
    online **248**.29
child poverty **235**.5, 18-22
    and child maintenance **257**.31
    and education **235**.21-2
    effects **235**.19
    quiz **235**.20
    statistics **235**.18-19
Child Poverty Act **235**.19
child prostitution **246**.27-8, 34-8
Child Protection Delivery Plan (CPDP) **248**.36
child protection
    global targets **248**.32-3
    legislation **248**.35-6
    services **248**.7-8
child safety orders **223**.32
Child Sex Offender Disclosure Scheme **248**.1, 35
child sexual exploitation **248**.30, 31; **268**.31, 32-4, 35-6
    definition **268**.32
child soldiers **259**.24; **268**.13, 14, 24-6

girls **259**.24
punishment **259**.24
under-18s recruitment into British army **268**.27
Child Support Agency **257**.30
child trafficking **268**.11, 31, 36-7
    and illegal adoption **268**.38-9
    sex trafficking **246**.35-7
childcare
    costs **257**.29
    and fathers **221**.4-5
    gender gap **221**.6
    need for reform **257**.31
    and welfare reform bill **235**.9
childhood, children's rights to **229**.25
childhood obesity **241**. 19, 35; **271**.8
    adoption of obese children **241**.23
    and Action on Sugar campaign **271**.20
    bariatric surgery **241**.22
    prevention **241**.19-21
childhood survival rate **251**.2
ChildLine **248**.7, 8, 16; **252**.15, 16
    number of calls **248**.2
children
    abuse *see* child abuse
    adopted
        contact with birth family **247**.16
        and education **247**.17
    and advertising **207**.35-6, 37, 39; **238**.6-7
        on social media **266**.24
    aggressive behaviour **224**.22-3
    anxiety and phobias **206**.13
    autism **255**.6
    and beauty pageants **238**.28-30
    as carers **255**.20-21
    causes of death **267**.20
    character skills, importance of **219**.34-5
    child-on-child sex attacks **238**.17; **248**.13
    and the commercial world **207**.37-9
    and crime **223**.30-32
        sentences for riot crime **223**.29
    and death of a pet **267**.9-10
    disabled *see* disabled children
    discipline **257**.24
    and divorce **244**.36-7
    and domestic abuse **224**.24-6, 37
    donor conceived **247**.39
    dyslexia indicators **255**.4-5
    and e-cigarette marketing **261**.12
    eating disorder **249**.3, 7-8, 21, 22
    faddy eating **249**.23-4
    family background, effect on outcomes **219**.22, 23, 25-6, 27-8, 29-30, 34
    family living arrangements, worldwide **257**.3-4
    financial awareness **250**.21
    and food additives **271**.10
    and fuel poverty **235**.15-16
    and funerals **267**.31
    and gambling **203**.12-14
        problem gambling **203**.20
    gender-variant behaviour **225**.23-4
    and healthy eating **271**.4
        eating same meals as parents **271**.30
        school meals **271**.34, 37-8

Tesco food education programme **271**.35-6
and HIV/AIDS **243**.23-5
cure of baby born with HIV **243**.37-9
infection rate reduction **243**.26-7
transmission from mother **243**.1-2
and homelessness **262**.6, 28
information held without parental consent **245**.16
injured by landmines **259**.39
and the Internet **230**.4-5, 25, 33-4; **245**.25-8; **266**.18, 20
and junk food marketing **271**.27-30
LGBT children and schools **225**.5-8
local authority responsibilities **224**.37
and mental health problems **201**.2-4
mental health support **258**.16
missing breakfast **271**.4
missing from care homes **248**.28
money worries **250**.20
National Child Measurement Programme **241**.24
obesity *see* childhood obesity
online privacy awareness **245**.25-6
and parental relationships
effects of parental separation **244**.36-7; **257**.12, 13
wellbeing effects of marriage **244**.10
and parental separation **201**.3; **244**.36-7; **257**.12, 13
parenting tips **257**.24
physical activity guidlines **241**.1, 6, 20
physical inactivity **241**.35
pocket money **250**.39
and poverty *see* child poverty
and prison *see* youth custody
rights of domestic abuse victims **224**.38
with same-sex parents **257**.14-15, 17
sexual abuse *see* sexual abuse
sexual exploitation risk for runaway children **262**.28
sexualisation of young children **221**.9-10; **238**.1-15, 27-36
and smoking **252**.37-9; **261**.6, 20
Indonesia **261**.38-9
passive smoking **252**.38; **261**.14, 28-9
and social media **266**.19, 20, 22-3
learning social networking skill **266**.25-6
parents monitoring **245**.26-7
and social mobility **219**.27
and sport **241**.35-6
as suicide bombers **212**.11-12
talking about suicide **258**.28
and tobacco marketing **261**.33
toy preferences and gender **221**.7-8
travel to school **200**.1-2, 19-20
undernourishment, developing countries **235**.26-7
unhappiness **258**.29
and vegetarian diet **214**.28, 36
victims of war **259**.25-6, 39
viewing Internet pornography **196**.38; **238**.3-4; **246**.10-11
and women's attitude to marriage **244**.6-7
of working mothers **221**.26
see also babies; boys and young men; girls and young women;
young people
CHILDREN 1ST **270**.28-9
Children Acts **248**.35
Children's Food Campaign **271**.29

children's rights **229**.24-6; **268**.13-30
to education **229**.24, 27-8
global trends **268**.19-20
UK **229**.29-30; **268**.17-19
see also UN Convention on the Rights of the Child China
child labour **268**.11
death penalty **229**.37
economic development **226**.21
Google withdrawing from China **196**.27-28, 29, 30
illegal adoption **268**.38
one-child rule **220**.4, 18
plastic waste import ban **242**.19
population trends **220**.8
poverty rates **235**.23
privacy rights **245**.4
Chinese herbal medicine
and dementia **269**.22
and depression **269**.24-5
chiropractic **269**.3, 8
chlamydia **237**.20, 22
rates in young people **252**.2, 3
testing for **237**.22, 24
chlorinating water, environmental impact **218**.38-9
cholesterol **271**.15-16
Choosing to Die documentary **217**.20
Choto-san (herbal medicine) **269**.22
CHP *see* combined heat and power
Christianity **215**.1-2
and abortion **231**.19
and Britain **215**.14
as default religion in Britain **215**.15-16
and equality legislation **215**.25
and the law **215**.26-7
and pornography **246**.1
and same sex marriage **244**.18
anad war and peace **259**.4-5
chronic obstructive pulmonary disease (COPD) **261**.8
Chunk the Junk survey **271**.37
church attendance **215**.6
Church of England and same sex marriage **244**.23-4
churches
and civil partnerships **244**.17
and marriage **244**.2, 4, 8-9
and same sex marriage **244**.23-4, 25
cigarettes
chemical content **261**.3
consumption trends **261**.6-7
in films **261**.18-19
marketing and children **261**.33, 39
packaging **261**.27, 35
purchase age, New York **261**.30
see also smoking; tobacco; tobacco industry
Cinematograph Films (Animals) Act **196**.14
CIRA (Continuity IRA) **212**.14
circuses, use of wild animals **233**.4, 14-15
CITES (Convention on International Trade in Endangered Species) **260**.27
cities *see* cars, congestion; urban areas; urban growth
Citizens Advice and debt help **250**.29-30
citizenship
citizenship lessons to include financial education **250**.19
and Muslims **215**.9-10

tests **220**.30-31; **240**.7
citizenship education **240**.1-2
    Youth Parliament manifesto **240**.38
civil marriage ceremonies **244**.2
civil partnerships **244**.16-18
    dissolution **244**.30-31
    legal equivalence with marriage **225**.35
    for opposite-sex couples **225**.33
    in religious buildings **225**.32; **244**.17
civil rights and children, England **268**.17
Claimant Commitment (Jobseekers Allowance) **263**.9
Claimant Count **263**.2
class see social class
classification
    of drugs **228**.21, 24, 25
        criticism of **228**.22-3
        designer drugs **228**.32-3
        reclassification of cannabis **228**.23; **256**.1, 27
    of films **196**.13-16
    of video games **196**.17
climate change **216**.1-39; **218**.19
    adaptation to **216**.28, 29-30
    and British weather **216**.4, 8, 9
    Cancun Agreement **226**.4
    controversies **216**.18-27
    definitions **216**.5
    effects of **216**.4, 6-7, 8, 9, 10-12, 14
    evidence for **216**.3, 5-6, 18-19, 20, 22-4
    and food production **214**.17, 18, 19, 21; **216**.6-7,
       10
    and forests **216**.14-15
    international agreements **216**.37-9; **226**.4
    measurement **216**.26-7
    and meat production **214**.17, 18, 19, 21
    mechanisms **216**.2
    and migration **220**.20, 28, 29
    mitigation **216**.7, 28
    political attitudes **216**.25
    predictions **216**.6, 9
    public attitudes **216**.21, 24, 25, 32; **218**.14
    refugees **216**.10-11
    and renewable energy sources
        microgeneration **204**.36
        wind energy **204**.12
    response to **216**.28-39
    scepticism **216**.23-4, 25
    and sea level **216**.9, 16-17, 20-21
    and tourism **222**.22
    UN rainforest protection initiative **218**.20-21
    and water resources **218**.33
    see also energy efficiency; global warming;
greenhouse gas emissions
climate events of 2010 **216**.13
climate forcing **216**.1
climate justice **218**.4
climate measurement **216**.26-7
climate models **216**.2
climate sensitivity **216**.2
Climbie, Victoria **248**.1
Clinical Commissioning Groups (CGCs) **251**.25, 29, 31
clinical (major) depression **265**.1
Clinton Global Initiative (CGI) **260**.24-5
cloning see animal cloning; human cloning

Close, Glenn, and sister's bipolar disorder **265**.9-10
closed list voting system **240**.29
clothes
    energy-harvesting **204**.39
    for a funeral **267**.31
    mourning **267**.12
clubs and societies at university **264**.22-3, 28-9
CO_2 see carbon dioxide
coal, production trends **204**.1
coastal areas
    effect of climate change **216**.7
    effects of tourism **222**.25
Coca-Cola, alcohol content **254**.34
code layer of privacy **245**.3
coercive control and domestic violence **224**.34-5
coffee shops and cannabis, The Netherlands **256**.31
coffins, costs **267**.34
cognitive behavioural therapy (CBT); **252**.15, 19
    and depression **265**.4, 24, 26, 27, 34, 36-7
    and phobias **206**.13
    and post traumatic stress disorder, armed forces
      213.34
    and problem gambling **203**.24
    and prolonged grief **267**.6-7
    and seasonal affective disorder **265**.11
    SPARX computer program **265**.36-7
    and stress **206**.3, 12
cognitive enhancing drugs **252**.33, 34
cohabitation
    after relationship breakdown **244**.38-9
    before marriage, and likelihood of divorce **244**.33
    break-up rates of cohabiting couples **257**.12
    global variations **257**.4-5
    see also common-law marriage
cola drinks, alcohol content **254**.34
Colombia, town banning tourists **222**.32
colour preferences and gender **221**.7-8
combination therapy for depression **265**.22
combined heat and power (CHP)
    and fuel cells **204**.38
    microgeneration **204**.35
combined pill **237**.6
commercial radio **210**.3
commercialisation, effect on children **207**.38-9
Commission on Funding of Care and Support
(Dilnot Report) **239**.20, 22-3
committees, Cabinet **240**.26
common law marriage **244**.8-9
    see also cohabitation
communication
    and family life **257**.24
    trends **210**.4-5
    see also media; telecommunications; telephones
Communications Data Bill **245**.5-8
    and Internet pornography **246**.8
    objections to **245**.6-7, 8
community heat networks **242**.33
community sentences **223**.20, 23
Community Service Volunteers (CSV) **240**.36
Company magazine, 'pro-skinny' article **249**.27
company boards see boardroom positions
company pensions **250**.12
Compassion in Dying information line **217**.37

compensation and the Human Rights Act **229**.5-6

complaints process, NHS **251**.26

complementary and alternative medicine (CAM) **269**.1-39

    and cancer **269**.6-9, 19, 28-30, 31

    choosing a practitioner **269**.8-9, 11, 21, 23

    definitions **269**.6, 7, 18

    and depression **252**.19; **265**.3, 11, 25

    and palliative care **269**.23

    popularity **269**.5-6, 11

    regulation **269**.1, 8-9, 16

        herbal medicines **269**.13-14, 15

        homeopathy **269**.12

    and seasonal affective disorder **265**.11

    types **269**.1-4, 6-7

    see also acupuncture; aromatherapy; Chinese

medicine; herbal medicine; homeopathy

complicated (prolonged) grief **267**.3-4, 6-7

composting waste **218**.11-12

    gas production **204**.24

comprehensive school pupils, degree performance

    209.12; **219**.32

comprehensive sexuality education **237**.38-9

compressed air energy storage (CAES) **204**.37-8

compulsive exercising **249**.7

compulsive gambling see problem gambling

compulsive shopping **207**.6

computed tomography (CT) scanners **251**.2

computer network attacks **196**.34

computers

    late-night use and depression **252**.20

    see also Internet

concentrating solar thermal power (CSP) **204**.3

conception problems see infertility

conception rate, UK **257**.10

    young people **252**.1, 3

condoms **237**.2, 3-4, 6, 18-19

    failure **237**.2, 6

    obtaining **237**.3-4, 19

    and the prevention of STIs **237**.18-19

    safe use **237**.2

    use in porn films **246**.5

conflict see war

conflict-induced displacement **220**.36-7; **259**.22

conflict minerals **226**.3

conflict model **259**.36-7

conflicts see war and conflict

congestion, traffic

    London Congestion Charge **200**.17-18

    public attitudes **200**.5-6

Congo, natural resources and violence **226**.3

Connelly, Peter (Baby P) **248**.1

consecutive sentences **223**.19

consent, sexual **237**.12-13

conservation, wildlife **260**.27-39

    see also endangered species; extinction

constitution, British, and Christianity **215**.14

construction, houses see house building

consumer power **207**.3-5

    and ethical consumerism **207**.23-4

consumer rights **207**.12-22

    credit card purchases **207**.12, 18

    online shopping **207**.12, 13

consumer spending see spending

consumer trends **207**.1-11

consumerism

    and children **207**.37-9

    problems **207**.2

consumers

    and energy industry **218**.10

    ethical shopping **226**.38

    and food from cloned animals **211**.11, 12, 14

    and GM foods **208**.29-30, 31, 33

    rights see consumer rights

    and sustainable development **226**.4

    see also shopping

consumption inequality and population growth

    220.11-12, 14, 15

contact orders and grandparents **257**.18-19, 20

contamination

    of crops by GM crops **208**.24, 27

    see also pollution

contraception **237**.2, 6-11

    developing countries **220**.16-17

    sources of information **237**.8-9

    see also condoms; family planning; pill,

contraceptive

contraceptive implants **237**.7

contraceptive injections **237**.7

Convention for the Protection of the World Cultural

and Natural Heritage **260**.27

Convention on Action against Trafficking in Human

Beings **246**.31-2

Convention on Biological Diversity (CBD) **260**.28

Convention on the Conservation of European

Wildlife and Natural Habitats **260**.27

Convention on the Conservation of Migratory

Species of Wild Animals **260**.27

Convention on International Trade in Endangered

Species of Wild Fauna and Flora (CITES) **260**.27

Convention on the Rights of the Child see UN

Convention on the Rights of the Child

conversion therapy (homosexuality) **225**.17-18

cookies (Internet) **245**.3, 9-10

cooking, children's experience of **271**.4

cooperation, global **226**.17-19, 22-5

Copenhagen climate change summit **216**.37, 38

copycat suicides **258**.26

copyright and the Internet **230**.30, 35-7

coral reefs, threats to **218**.24

coronary heart disease (CHD) see heart disease

Corporate Social Responsibility **207**.30; **226**.38;

    227.9-10, 12, 18-19

correspondence rights **245**.1

cortisol **206**.30

    as biomarker for depression **265**.14

cosmetics industry, mica mining and child labour **268**.7-9

cosmetic surgery

    desire for **234**.14-15, 19, 33

    Girlguiding UK campaign **234**.34

    regulation **234**.21

cost of living rising faster than earnings **207**.8

costs

    of ageing population **239**.15

    alcohol

        minimum unit pricing **254**.14, 19, 37-8

        costs to society **254**.21

    care for the elderly **239**.20-23

    CCTV **245**.28-9

climate change **216**.4
communications service **210**.10, 14-15
domestic violence **224**.27
drug abuse **228**.1-2, 24
of eating disorders **249**.
education **235**.21, 22
ethical food labelling **207**.29
of family breakdown **257**.12
of fraud **207**.21-2
funerals **267**.34-5
higher education **264**.9, 11, 12
holidays **222**.5, 6-7
of mental ill health **201**.1, 5, 23
of the NHS **251**.8
of obesity and overweight **241**.3, 18-19
organic food **207**.30
of physical inactivity **241**.1-2
prohibiting couples from divorce and separation **244**.33, 38-9
of raising a disabled child **255**.8
smoking **261**.9, 21, 26
vegetarian food **214**.12
wind farms **204**.17-18
of work-related stress **206**.5
Côte d'Ivoire, use of drone **259**.13
Council of Europe
Convention on Action against Trafficking in Human Beings **246**.31-2
convention on domestic violence **224**.32-3
council tax **250**.14
councils see local authorities
counselling
abortion **231**.24-5, 26-9, 31, 36-7
for alcohol dependence **254**.9
for children **258**.16
couples unable to afford **244**.38
for depression **239**.31; **252**.15. 19; **265**.4, 24, 26, 29
for postnatal depression **265**.13
for self-harm **258**.3, 14, 15
and help with stress **206**.2
counter-terrorism **212**.15-25
legislation **212**.19, 20
police powers **212**.15-16
Prevent strategy **212**.17-18
UK strategy review **212**.21-2, 26, 38-9
Counter Terrorism Act 2008 **212**.19
counterfeit alcohol **254**.13, 38
couple-focused therapy and depression **265**.26
courtesy stigma **255**.26
courts, support for sexual abuse victims **248**.39
cows see cattle
crabs (pubic lice) **237**.21
cranberries as natural remedy **269**.27
creationism teaching at free school **215**.22
credit
consumer credit levels **207**.16
credit files **207**.20
credit ratings **250**.9, 10
logbook loans **235**.12
payday loans **235**.11
see also debt
credit cards
and consumer rights **207**.12, 18

fraud **223**.4
credit crunch see recession
credit unions **235**.11
cremation
costs **267**.34
and death certificates **267**.28-9
of a pet **267**.9
cricket players visiting schools **270**.7
crime **223**.1-18
against disabled people **255**.11
and aggressive behaviour in children **224**.23
causes of criminal behaviour **223**.11
rioting **223**.8, 9-10
and CCTV **245**.29, 30, 31
committed by children **223**.30-31
and Communications Data Bill **245**.5
crime mapping **223**.1-2
crimes against humanity **259**.28
cybercrime **230**.29
and DNA evidence **245**.14, 15
and gangs **223**.6-7, 13-15
HIV transmission as crime **243**.11
and household insurance **235**.7
knife crime **223**.5
prevention **223**.6-7, 16-17, 34
punishment **223**.21, 25
levels of crime **223**.2, 3-5
and mental health sufferers **201**.22
phishing **230**.30
reporting a crime **223**.12
riots **223**.8-11
and slums **235**.37
victims of see victims of crime
war crimes **259**.8, 24, 28
waste crime **242**.8-9, 10-12
see also fraud; victims of crime; violent crime; young offenders
Crime and Courts Bill **248**.34
crime prevention **223**.12-18
and CCTV **245**.29, 30, 31
gangs and youth violence **223**.7, 13-15, 35-6
role of ex-offenders **223**.18
and schools **223**.16-17
Criminal Justice Act and hate crime **225**.31
Criminal Justice and Immigration Act **196**.14
and pornography **246**.8
Criminal Justice and Police Act, and prostitution **246**.18
criminal justice system **223**.19-39
and children **223**.29, 30-32
and ethnic minorities **236**.9, 10
gang injunctions **223**.35-6
reforms **223**.24-5
restorative justice **223**.28-9
sentencing **223**.19-22, 23, 33
see also prison
criminal responsibility, age of **223**.30
reasons for raising **223**.31-2
criminalisation of demand for prostitution **246**.20
impact on sex trafficking **246**.33
criminalisation of homelessness **262**.18
criminalisation of homosexuality, globally **225**.39
criminals
and the Human Rights Act **229**.5, 6

stereotyping of homeless people **262**.14
see also prisoners
Crisis **262**.21
Croatia, smoking ban **261**.31
Crohn's disease, cannabis treatment **256**.20
crop biotechnology *see* genetically modified (GM) crops
cross-contamination, GM crops **208**.24, 26
crossdressers **225**.19
crowdsourcing CCTV monitoring **245**.30
cruise ships, impact on environment **222**.25
cryopreservation *see* freezing
crystal meth (methamphetamine) **228**.23
CSE (comprehensive sexuality education) **237**.38-9
CSP (concentrating solar thermal power) **204**.3
CSV (Community Service Volunteers) **240**.36
Cuba, reversing obesity problem **271**.9
cultural identity
British *see* British identity
culture
and age discrimination **239**.6-7
and body image **234**.3
British **240**.3, 14
and child labour **268**.3-4
effect of tourism **222**.22, 29, 30
of worklessness **263**.6, 13-14
Cura (website for carers) **239**.38
curriculum
and faith schools **215**.19
reform **209**.5
custody *see* prison; youth custody
customer service lines **207**.14
credit card companies **207**.17-18
cutting *see* self-harm
CVD *see* cardiovascular disease
cyber stalking **230**.23
cyberbullying **230**.23; **232**.2, 25-39
dealing with **232**.3, 26, 29, 39
effects **232**.25, 26
forms **232**.25
prevalence **232**.30, 31; **265**.18
preventing **230**.28; **232**.26-7, 28
reasons for **232**.25-6
reporting **232**.29
and teenage suicides **258**.36-7
at work **227**.38
cybercrime **230**.29
cycling **200**.21
bicycle security at university **264**.17
cycles sharing roads with cars **200**.18
impact of traffic **200**.16
to school **200**.1-2
Cyclone Technologies **255**.33
Cyprus, smoking ban **261**.31
Czech Republic smoking ban **261**.31

D

D&E (surgical dilation and evacuation) **231**.7
dairy farming, mega-dairies **233**.9-10
dairy foods *see* milk
dancing, health benefits for older people **241**.33-4
Dangerous Dogs Act **233**.4, 12-13

dark tourism **222**.16
Darwin, Charles, on homeopathy **269**.32
Data Communications Bill *see* Communications Data Bill
Data Protection Act **245**.11
data protection laws, worldwide **245**.4
date labels on food packaging **242**.14, 15
dead zones, oceans **218**.24-5
deafness **239**.25
Death Cafes **267**.11
death penalty **223**.37-9; **229**.37-8
and European Court of Human Rights **229**.39
deaths
AIDS-related **243**.6, 26, 27
in armed conflicts **259**.6
in Armed Forces **213**.9
of babies **267**.21-2
beliefs about **267**.23
causes of **267**.20, 21, 22
drug-related **228**.2, 13
cannabis **256**.8, 36
dying **267**.18-19
earlier death
of mental health sufferers **201**.26
of people with learning difficulties **255**.3
from eating disorders **249**.5, 16
funerals *see* funerals
of homeless people **262**.20-21, 32
legal rights and responsibilities **267**.28-30
memorials *see* remembrance of the deceased
older people, risk increased by loneliness **239**.36-7
of pets **267**.8-10
registering **267**.28
talking about death **267**.11, 24-5, 27
thinking about death, benefits of **267**.26
see also bereavement; euthanasia; mortality
debt
advice **250**.29-30, 31, 33, 37-8
buying on credit **207**.6, 16
developing world **226**.5-6
families **257**.25
health impacts **250**.29, 33
levels of debt **250**.5, 11, 32
students **209**.31-2; **264**.20, 29
debt cancellation, developing countries **226**.5-6
debt crisis **226**.5
Declaration of Internet Freedom **230**.37
decriminalisation
of cannabis **256**.21, 30-31, 38
of drugs possession **228**.34
of prostitution **246**.20
defence
budget cuts **213**.17-19, 20-21, 22-3, 28
see also Armed Forces
deforestation
dryland forests **218**.21
by palm oil industry, and Sumatran tigers **260**.12
rainforest protection programme **218**.20-21
and tobacco production **261**.9
degrees, university **264**.1
costs and benefits **264**.11, 12
sponsored **264**.1, 3
and students' school background **209**.12; **219**.32

dementia **239**.4, 5, 28-9
   as cause of death **267**.20
   complementary and alternative therapies **269**.20-22
   and depression **201**.12-13
   worries about **239**.30
   in younger people **201**.10-11
   see also Alzheimer's disease
dementia services **201**.5, 10-11
democracy
   and Islam **215**.10
   see also electoral systems
Democratic Republic of the Congo, use of drones **259**.13
demographic transition **220**.3
demographics *see* population; population growth
demonstrations via the Internet **196**.32
Denmark, energy from waste **242**.33
dental dams **237**.18-19
Department of Health **251**.30
Depaul UK **262**.23, 26, 27
dependency
   on alcohol **254**.1-2, 8-9
     drug prescriptions **254**.10
     and minimum unit pricing **254**.38
   on cannabis **256**.6, 8, 12
     definitions **256**.17, 23
     signs **256**.14
     user characteristics **256**.15-16
   on cigarette smoking **261**.7
   on drugs
     cannabis as gateway drug **256**.8, 34, 37
     cannabis as substitute **256**.18
   on synthetic cannabinoids **256**.4
   see also addictions
deportation of non-nationals, and Human Rights Act **229**.4-5
depressant drugs (downers) **228**.3
   see also cannabis; heroin; solvents
depression **239**.24-5; **265**.1-18
   antidepressant drugs *see* antidepressant drugs
   and cannabis use **256**.11
   causes of **265**.1
   in children and young people **252**.18-19; **258**.16; **265**.
     16-17
   and Chinese herbal medicine **269**.24-5
   as a disability **265**.5
   and dementia **201**.12-13; **239**.32
   and eating disorders **249**.3
   and fast food **252**.24
   and grief **267**.4, 8
   and HIV diagnosis **243**.13, 31
   and late night screen use **252**.20; **265**.13
   and malnutrition **271**.5
   manic depression *see* bipolar affective disorder
   and older people **239**.31-2
     living with HIV **243**.31
   as physical illness **265**.8
   post-natal **265**.2, 12-13
   and suicide **258**.26-7
   symptoms **239**.31; **265**.1
     post-natal depression **265**.12
   treatments **239**.31; **265**.19-37
     cognitive behavioural therapy **265**.4, 24, 26, 27, 34, 36-7
     complementary medicine **265**.3, 11, 25
     Seasonal Affective Disorder **265**.11

     self-help **239**.31-2; **265**.2
     young people **265**.17; 36-7
     see also antidepressant drugs
   types of **265**.1-2
   young people **252**.18-19; **265**.16-17
     and antidepressants **265**.21-2
     treatment using SPARX computer program **265**.
      36-7
     unemployed **252**.21; **265**.15
   see also bipolar affective disorder, (manic depression);
     seasonal affective disorder (SAD)
deprivation
   and homelessness **262**.24
   and malnutrition **271**.5
   and obesity **271**.8
designer drugs, control of **228**.32-3
detention
   of children **268**.14, 18-19
   of terrorist suspects **212**.16
   see also prison
detoxification from alcohol dependence **254**.9
developed countries, impact of globalization **226**.
   24-5
developing countries
   age structures **220**.8
   aid to *see* aid
   biofuels causing food shortages **204**.33-4
   and climate change **216**.11
   and contraception **220**.16-17
   debt **226**.5-6
   definition **226**.30
   education **209**.8; **229**.27-8
   fertility rates **220**.2, 3, 4, 12, 13
   and free trade **226**.32, 33-4
   gender inequality **221**.1-2, 35
   girls' education **221**.35, 38-9; **229**.27-8
   and globalisation **226**.3-4
   and GM crops **208**.10
   and ICT **230**.7
   loans for small businesses **235**.33-5
   and population growth **220**.2, 4, 5-7
   and poverty **235**.23-39
   poverty reduction strategies **235**.24
   remittances from migrant workers **220**.35
   and renewable energy **204**.2
   slum tourism **222**.16, 33-4
   and transport **200**.13
   UK trade initiatives **226**.28
   World Bank support **226**.9-10
   and World Trade Organization **226**.8
   see also Millennium Development Development
Goals
development-induced displacement **220**.37; **259**.22
Devil's in Your Details campaign **245**.22
devolved government **240**.27-8
diabetes **239**.25; **241**.3
   and bulimia (diabulimia) **249**.11
   in children and young people **252**.8
   and meat consumption **214**.35
   prevalence **241**.3, 9
diary of grieving **267**.13
diet

children **252**.29
and depression **265**.3, 11, 24-5
healthy *see* healthy eating
macrobiotic **269**.4
and malnutrition **271**.5
and mental health **252**.24, 25
and overweight **241**.15-16
and seasonal affective disorder **265**.11
and stress **206**.33
Victorian **271**.1-2
young people **252**.4
see also dieting; eating disorders; food and
nutrition; healthy eating; veganism; vegetarianism
diet industry **234**.7-8
dietary obsession (orthorexia nervosa) **249**.8
dietary supplements
and alcohol dependence **254**.9
and malnutrition **271**.5
and vegetarian diet **214**.10, 29
dieting and body image **234**.12
digital dating abuse **224**.20
digital fluency **230**.10-12
digital footprints **230**.31-2; **266**.7, 18
digital legacy **267**.37-8
digital literacy **230**.13
digital natives **230**.8-9
digital radio **210**.15
digital technology
and homeless people **262**.34-5
see also computers; Internet; mobile phones
digital travel **266**.32-3
Dignity in Dying **217**.38
criticism of assisted suicide policy **217**.26
dilation and evacuation (abortion) **231**.7
Dilnot Commission on Funding of Care and Support
239.20, 22-3
diplomas, gender-stereotypical choices **221**.28
direct discrimination
against Gypsies and Travellers **236**.22
racial **236**.1-2
sexual orientation **225**.28
directors, company *see* boardroom positions
disability **255**.1-39
and abortion **231**.20
autistic spectrum disorders **255**.3, 6-8
benefit reform **255**.34; **263**.8, 9
definitions **255**.1, 2
and employment **255**.3, 22-3, 29, 31, 32-3
learning disabilities **255**.2
and mental health, young people **201**.3
and older people **239**.4; **255**.22-3
see also disabled children; disabled people
Disability Confident campaign **255**.32
Disability Discrimination Act
and depression **265**.5
and workplace stress **206**.28
Disability Employment Conference **255**.32-3
Disability Living Allowance **255**.41; **263**.9
and benefit scrounger rhetoric **255**.10-11, 37
disability rights **255**.29-39
education **255**.29-30
and police interviews **255**.30
at work **255**.29
disabled children

costs **255**.8
parents experiencing stigma **255**.25-8
disabled people **255**.1-28
and assisted suicide **217**.19, 21
attitudes to **255**.10-11, 25-8, 37
being labelled **255**.9
benefit cuts **229**.32; **255**.34, 35, 38
benefit reforms **255**.34; **263**.8, 9
benefit scrounger rhetoric **255**.10-11, 37
definition **255**.1, 41
discrimination *see* Disability discrimination Act
and domestic abuse **224**.4
and employment **255**.3, 22-3, 29, 31, 32-3
exercise and fitness **255**.14-15
and financial insecurity **263**.16
in low-income households **235**.5, 7
older people **255**.22-3
Paralympic Games impact **255**.15-16, 17; **270**.
12-13
participation in decision-making **255**.12-13
people with learning disabilities **255**.2-3
housing **255**.13-14
and police interviews **255**.30
public perceptions of **255**.10-11, 25-8, 37
and sport **255**.14-15; **270**.3, 12-13, 14
see also disability; learning disabilities
disaster-induced displacement **220**.37; **259**.22-3
disaster tourism **222**.16
discipline of children **257**.25
discrimination
anti-discrimination legislation **221**.3, 36
and workplace stress **206**.28-9
against Christians **215**.25
definition **221**.3
and depression **265**.5, 6-7
Disability Discrimination Act and workplace stress **206**.28
gender discrimination at work **221**.18, 23-4
see also gender pay gap
against HIV sufferers **243**.15, 16-17
against Muslims **215**.30, 31-2
racial *see* racial discrimination
religious **215**.23-4; 30; 31-2
and same sex marriage views **244**.24, 25
sexual orientation **225**.9-10, 28-9
and religious beliefs **225**.35
in sport **270**.9, 24-5
in the workplace **215**.23-4; **221**.18, 23-4
see also prejudice; racism; sex discrimination
discussion boards **266**.1
disease
resistance, GM crops **208**.1, 29
stem cell treatment **211**.30, 36-7, 38-9
disordered eating **249**.10
displaced people *see* refugees
divorce **244**.30-39
and alcohol consumption **244**.32
benefits **244**.37
divorce rate **244**.31
and children's mental health **201**.3
grounds for **244**.30
risk factors **244**.32-3
see also parental separation; separation
DNA **208**.7; **211**.3; **245**.14
DNA database **245**.14-15

Do Not Attempt Resuscitation (DNAR) order **217**.3, 14

docking dogs' tails **233**.6

doctors
    and abortion **231**.2, 25, 28, 29, 32-3
    and assisted suicide **217**.4, 8, 11, 22, 24-5, 31
    impact of legalizing assisted dying **217**.4, 8, 11, 31
    on restricting treatment of smokers and obese people **261**.22-3
    see also GPs (general practitioners); physician-assisted
        suicide (PAS)

dodo extinction **260**.3

Dog Control Bill **233**.4

doggy box scheme, restaurants **242**.39

dogs
    and animal rights **233**.4
    Dangerous Dogs Act **233**.4, 12-13
    tail docking **233**.6

Dolly the sheep **211**.7, 8

dolphins
    dolphin-watching holidays **222**.26
    rights **233**.20

domestic abuse **224**.1-39
    costs **224**.27
    definitions **224**.1, 34-7
    excuses for **224**.1-2
    help for perpetrators **224**.39
    help for victims **224**.38
    and homelessness **262**.2, 7
    impact on children **224**.24-6, 37
    lesbian, gay, bisexual and transgender relationships **224**.5, 12-13
    male victims **224**.5, 9-10, 11
    and mental health of children **201**.3
    myths **224**.6-7
    personal stories **224**.8, 21, 26
    prevalence of **224**.28
    prevention strategy **224**.28-31
    signs of abuse
      in children **224**.24, 25
      in teenagers **224**.16-17
    statistics **224**.11
    staying with an abusive partner **224**.6
    support for victims **224**.38
    and young people **224**.4, 16-26

domestic waste *see* household waste

domestic workers and human trafficking **229**.18

donor insemination **247**.7-8
    giving information to children **247**.39

'don't ask don't tell' policy, US military **225**.38-9

doping *see* drugs in sport

Dove, self-esteem campaign **234**.33

downers *see* depressant drugs

Down's syndrome **255**.3

drag queens/kings **225**.19

Drax power plant, biomass fuel **204**.5, 7

drink-driving **254**.16

drinking water access **218**.31-3, 36

driving
    and alcohol *see* drink-driving
    and cannabis use **256**.4, 11
    dementia sufferers **201**.11
    and drugs **256**.4
    motorway phobia **200**.4

drones **259**.12, 13

drought **218**.23

drug abuse **228**.1-39
    costs **228**.1-2, 24
    deaths from **228**.2, 13; **252**.32
    declining **228**.35
    drug education campaign **228**.10-11
    effects **228**.12-13
    and HIV **243**.7
    and homeless people **262**.14
    ketamine **228**.5
    legal highs **228**.1, 36-8; **252**.32
    needle sharing and HIV transmission **243**.1
    signs of **228**.14-15
    statistics **228**.1, 13, 35
    smart drugs **252**.33, 34
    treatment **228**.16-18
    trends **228**.1
    types of drugs **228**.3-4
    young people **252**.1, 31, 32, 35
    see also cannabis

drug development and animal experiments *see* animal experiments

drug gangs, targeted by National Crime Agency **223**.22

drug overdoses, emergency treatment **228**.2

drug policy **228**.24-7
    and designer drugs **228**.32-3
    need for review **228**.39
    see also classification of drugs

drug treatments
    for alcohol dependence **254**.10
    for depression *see* antidepressant drugs
    for gambling addiction **203**.27

drugs
    animal research in drug development **233**.30-33
    for assisted dying, availability **217**.34
    cannabis *see* cannabis
    classification **228**.21, 24, 25
      cannabis **256**.1, 27
      criticism of **228**.22-3
    decriminalisation campaign **228**.34
    definition **228**.21
    effects **228**.4, 12-20
      cannabis **256**.2, 11-26
    fertility drugs **247**.8-9
    government policies **228**.24-7
    and the law **228**.21-39; **228**.13, 21-39
      cannabis **256**.1-2, 27-39
    types **228**.3-4
    see also cannabis; drug abuse; medicines

drugs in sport
    anabolic steroids **270**.30-31
    dangers **270**.31-2
    drug testing as invasion of privacy **270**.9

drunk tank **254**.15

drunkorexia **254**.33-4

dryland forests **218**.21

Duke of Edinburgh's Award **240**.37

dumping (trade) **226**.30, 32

dumping of waste, illegal **242**.8-9, 10, 12

dyscalculia **255**.5

dyslexia **255**.4-5

E

e-bullying *see* cyberbullying
e-cigarettes **261**.11-12, 13, 25, 37
    reasons for use **261**.11-12, 37
    safety **261**.11, 13
    and Tobacco Product Directive **261**.27
e-mail *see* email
E-number food additives **271**.10
e-reader accounts after death **267**.38
early onset dementia **201**.10-11
early years education *see* foundation stage
education
earnings
    attitudes to wage levels **219**.15
    gender gap *see* gender pay gap
    graduates **263**.25; **264**.11
    National Minimum Wage **263**.5-6
    statistics **263**.27
    see also incomes; salaries; wages
Eastern European migrants, UK **220**.24-5
    as victims of racism **236**.32
Eat Happy Project, Tesco **271**.35-6
eating disorders **249**.1-39
    causes **249**.2-3, 17-18, 21, 32
    children **249**.3, 7-8, 21, 22
    as effect of child abuse **248**.4-5
    effects **249**.5, 14
    getting help **249**.4, 5, 20, 21, 34
    and the media **249**.15, 25-31
    prevalence **249**.4, 15-16
    self-help **249**.3-4
    treatments **249**.32-9
    see also anorexia nervosa; bulimia nervosa;
obesity
eating habits
    students **209**.32, 33
    see also diet; healthy eating
eatwell plate **271**.25, 39
ebony forest regeneration by giant tortoises **260**.39
ECO (Energy Company Obligation) **253**.35
eco-housing **216**.29-30
eco-lodges **222**.24
eco-towns **253**.36
Ecominds **241**.12
economic (financial) abuse **224**.3
economic growth
    Brazil **226**.20-21
    China **226**.21
    and globalisation **226**.3-4
    impact of climate change **216**.11-12
    impact of population growth **220**.7
    need for international cooperation **226**.17-19
    role of business **227**.14
    and welfare spending **263**.8
economy
    recession *see* recession
    and tourism **222**.28, 30
        Britain **222**.4-5
ecosystems

biodiversity **218**.18
    impact of climate change **216**.6
    restoration (rewilding) **260**.34-5, 36-7, 39
    role of rhinos and elephants **260**.11
ecotourism **222**.8-9, 22-3, 24-5, 27-8
ecstasy (MDMA), signs of use **228**.14
ectopic pregnancy risk in IVF **247**.7
Editor's Code (Press Complaints Commission) **210**.
    27-8
EDNOS (eating disorder not otherwise specified) **249**.7
education **209**.1-39
    and adopted children **247**.17
    barriers to **268**.3, 13-14
    and body image **234**.11, 21, 29-30
    and child labour **268**.12, 22-3
    and child poverty **235**.21-2
    children's rights **229**.24-5
    citizenship **240**.1-2, 38
    in developing countries **209**.8; **229**.27-8
    and disabled students **255**.29-30
        Uganda **255**.39
    on drugs, campaign for **228**.10-11
    early years, and social mobility **219**.17-18, 34-5
    and employment readiness **263**.20, 21-2
    enterprise education **263**.28-9
    and ethnic minorities **236**.10
    faith-based schools **215**.17-22
    financial **250**.17, 19, 21
    on food and nutrition **271**.4
        Tesco programme **271**.35-6
    girls
        barriers to education **221**.35, 38-9
        and child marriage **268**.29-30
        and population control **220**.7
    global gender inequality **221**.1, 35
    higher education *see* higher education;
universities
    about HIV/AIDS **243**.10-11
    as a human right **268**.13-14
    ICT skills **230**.13
    Millennium Development Goals **218**.39; **229**.27-8
    mobile-based learning, young mothers in Kenya **257**.
        38-9
    about online privacy **245**.26
    and peace **259**.37
    about pornography **246**.12-14
    and poverty **235**.21-2; **268**.18
    and professional sports players **270**.8
    and racism **236**.15, 16
    and relationship abuse **224**.17
    and sexualisation of children **238**.4, 11, 14
    single-sex schools **221**.30-32
    and social mobility **219**.17-18, 22, 23, 25-6, 27-8, 34-5
    and social networking **266**.25-6
    special educational needs (SEN) **255**.30
    and teenage pregnancy **257**.32
    see also educational achievement; schools; sex
education; students; teachers; universities
Education and Inspection Act 2006 **225**.7
education-to-employment path **263**.21-3
educational achievement
    and bullying **232**.8
    and cannabis use **256**.11

and child poverty **235**.21

degree level, and school background **209**.12; **219**.32

and environmental behaviour **218**.9

and importance of British identity **240**.20

on same sex marriage **244**.21, 24

and parental support **219**.33

and socio-economic background **209**.13-14; **219**.22, 23, 25-6, 27-8, 29-30, 34

standards improving **209**.7-10

statistics **235**.6

terrorist suspects **212**.9

white British pupils, effect of social class **219**.29-30

see also exam results

Educational Maintenance Allowance (EMA) **209**.17, 18

EEA (European Environment Agency) **200**.22

egg donation for research cloning **211**.30

Egypt, girls' education **229**.27-8

Ehrlich, Paul **220**.11

El Niño, impact on Galapagos penguins **260**.38

elderly people *see* older people

electoral systems **240**.29

electric buses **200**.28-9

electric cars **200**.26, 27; **204**.7

electricity markets, Europe **204**.11-12

electronic cigarettes *see* e-cigarettes

electronic waste **242**.20-21

EU exports **242**.19

illegal trade **218**.15-16

elephant poaching **260**.9-11, 21, 23

elevated water storage **204**.38

Elizabeth II (Queen) **240**.22-3

EMA (Educational Maintenance Allowance) **209**.17, 18

email

and bullying **232**.25

email accounts after death **267**.38

security **232**.27

support for anxiety sufferers **252**.14-15

embargoes on arms trade **259**.10

embedded water **218**.35

embryo cloning *see* human reproductive cloning

embryo splitting **211**.24

embryonic stem cells **211**.28, 29-30, 35-6

see also therapeutic cloning

embryos

moral status **211**.31, 34

and stem cell research **211**.31-2

EMDR (Eye Movement Desensitizing and Reprocessing) **213**.34

emergency accommodation **262**.7

emergency contraception **237**.2

emergency treatment, drug abuse **228**.2

emissions

reduction **200**.15

standards **200**.15

transport **200**.14, 22

see also greenhouse gas emissions

Emissions Trading Scheme and airlines **222**.14-15

emotional abuse **224**.1, 3

and children's mental health **201**.3

emotional distress and eating disorders **249**.3

emotional effects

of child abuse **248**.3, 4, 17, 26

of parental separation **257**.12, 13

emotional impact of HIV diagnosis **243**.12, 18

emotional neglect **248**.3

emotional signs of stress **206**.9, 19

emotions

British characteristics **267**.4-5

and death of a pet **267**.8-9

and grief **267**.1-2, 3

employees, gay and lesbian **225**.9

employers

involvement in schools **219**.26; **263**.27

links with universities **209**.29

potential use of social networks data **245**.23-4

views on qualifications **209**.3

and young people **263**.22, 26-7

employment

and age discrimination **239**.6, 12-13

and benefits reduction **263**.7

black students' employment prospects **236**.19-20

and childcare costs **257**.29

dementia sufferers **201**.11

difficulty finding jobs **235**.6

of disabled people **255**.22-3, 31, 32-3

disability rights **255**.29

people with learning disabilities **255**.3

ethnic pay gap **236**.18

ethnic minorities **236**.10-11

ex-offenders **223**.26-7

ex-service personnel **213**.32

and free trade **226**.13-14

and gender **221**.1-2, 18, 19, 27-9, 37

and globalisation **226**.22

graduates **263**.24-5; **264**.32-4

finding a job **264**.35, 37

unpaid work **264**.36-7, 38

and homelessness **262**.14-15, 39

international labour standards **229**.14-16

living wage for garment workers **229**.13

and mental health sufferers **201**.11, 22-3, 27

Millennium Development Goal **235**.26

migrant workers *see* migrant workers

money worries, impact on work **250**.33

National Insurance **250**.15

and online reputation **230**.32

past retirement age **239**.16, 18

and population growth **220**.6

by private sector businesses **227**.4

and race discrimination **236**.20

rights *see* employment rights

students **250**.24

tourism industry **222**.21, 30

Britain **222**.4

youth training scheme **222**.31

workplace pensions **250**.12

young people **263**.19-30

see also hours of work; jobs; part-time jobs; unemployment; women in the workforce; work-life balance; workplace bullying; workplace stress

Employment Assistance Programmes (EAPs) **206**.27

employment rights **263**.4-5

disability rights **255**.29

international standards **229**.14-16

and religious belief **215**.23-4

and voluntary work **264**.38
Employment and Support Allowance (ESA) **263**.9
empty homes **253**.18, 32-5
empty shops **207**.9
enacted stigma
　　about disabled children **255**.26-7
　　about HIV **243**.16
End of Life Assistance (Scotland) Bill **217**.30
end-of-life care, Liverpool Care Pathway **251**.15
end-of-life rights information line **217**.37
End Violence Against Women (EVAW) Coalitition **224**.31
endangered species **260**.1-3, 5, 22
　　bats **260**.1, 7
　　conservation work by zoos **233**.25, 26
　　large carnivores **260**.6
　　tigers **260**.1, 12
　　wildlife tourism **222**.26
　　see also extinction; wildlife
endometriosis **247**.2
energy **204**.1-39
　　and consumer choice **218**.10
　　energy companies, human rights considerations **229**.9
　　energy policies
　　　　EU **204**.30-31
　　　　UK **204**.7-8, 28-9
　　industry trends **204**.1
　　microgeneration **204**.35
　　power outage warnings via social media **266**.39
　　renewable see renewable energy
　　saving through recycling **242**.24
　　storage **204**.37
　　from waste **242**.32-3, 37
　　see also fuel poverty
Energy Company Obligation (ECO) **253**.35
energy consumption **204**.1
energy efficiency
　　costs **253**.35
　　in the home **235**.16
　　of housing stock **253**.1
　　and sustainable housing **253**.37
　　see also renewable energy
Engagement and Support Orders, sex workers **246**.21
England
　　abortion law **231**.3
　　devolution **240**.28
　　health and physical activity **241**.1-4
　　housing priority need definition **262**.3
　　smoking ban **261**.31
English people and national identity **240**.6, 8, 12, 18
enterprise education **263**.28-9
entertainment industry and ethnic minorities **236**.12
entrepreneurship
　　aspirations **227**.6
　　challenges to **227**.8
　　developing countries **235**.33-5
　　education **263**.28-9
　　government initiative **227**.7
　　young people **264**.10-11
environment
　　and agriculture **214**.16, 17,18-19, 21, 22, 23, 26
　　definition **218**.1
　　environmental causes of migration **220**.20, 38, 39
　　sustainable housing **253**.36, 37
　　and vegetarianism **214**.15-27

see also environmental impact; sustainable development; wildlife
environmental funerals **267**.36
environmental governance, international **260**.27-8
environmental impact
　　biodegradable products **218**.37
　　biofuels **204**.33-4
　　chemical pollutants **218**.38-9
　　free trade **226**.32
　　GM crops **208**.20-21, 22, 29
　　globalisation **226**.4
　　meat production **214**.18-19, 20-21; 23
　　non-agricultural market access (NAMA) **226**.15-16
　　plastic bags **242**.26-7
　　population growth **218**.26-7, 28; **220**.4, 6-7, 14
　　smoking **261**.9
　　tourism **222**.21, 22, 25, 27, 28, 29
　　transport **200**.1, 14-15, 16, 22, 24-5
　　　　reducing **200**.15, 19-20, 25
　　waste incineration **242**.34
environmental justice **218**.3-4
environmental retailing **207**.34
environmental sustainability see sustainability
environmental tobacco smoke see passive smoking
environmental tourism see ecotourism
epilepsy in children and young people **252**.8
EPO (erythropoietin) **270**.31
Equal Love campaign **225**.33
equal pay see gender pay gap
Equal Pay Act **221**.35-6
equality
　　and faith schools **215**.18-19, 20
　　in families **257**.7
　　legislation and religious belief **215**.25
Equality Act 2010 **221**.3, 36
　　definition of disabled person **255**.1, 41
　　and LGBT people in schools **225**.6
　　and mental health **201**.31
Equality and Human Rights Commission **229**.34
equatorial penguins **260**.38-9
equity loans **253**.7-8, 9
erythropoietin (EPO) **270**.31
ESA (Employment and Support Allowance) **263**.9
eSports tournaments **270**.34-6
essential fatty acids **271**.14
Essentials magazine, diversity award **234**.38
ethical consumerism **207**.23-39; **226**.38
　　statistics **207**.24
ethical food, labelling costs **207**.29
ethical investment and tax compliance **227**.33
ethical tourism see ecotourism; responsible travel; sustainable tourism
ethical trade see fair trade
Ethical Trading Initiative (ETI) **226**.27
ethical volunteering **222**.38-9
ethics
　　and abortion **231**.16-29
　　and animal cloning **211**.10
　　and biotechnology **211**.6
　　of euthanasia and assisted suicide **217**.1-23
　　of human cloning **211**.8-9, 26-7
　　and stem cell research **211**.30-31, 34
　　and tourism industry **222**.31-2

Ethiopia, girls' education and child marriage **244**.15
ethnic cleansing **259**.28
ethnic diversity, Britain **240**.15-16
ethnic equality, public opinion **229**.12
ethnic minorities
    and British identity **240**.18-20
    and employment **236**.10-11, 20
    life in Britain **236**.6-12
    and low income households **235**.7-8
    and mental health problems **201**.2
    women and poverty **221**.34
    see also Asian people; black people; employment
and racism; racism
ethnic origin
    British population **240**.15-16
    poverty and educational achievement **209**.13-14
    and sport participation **270**.2
ethnic pay gap **236**.18
ethnic stereotypes
    reducing through tourism **222**.30
Europe
    attitudes to biotechnology **211**.5-6
    cannabis users **256**.15-16
    domestic violence treaty **224**.32-3
    internally displaced persons **259**.18
    Internet trade in wildlife **260**.17-18
    and LGBT equality **225**.39
    press freedom **196**.2
    smoking bans **261**.31-2
    see also European Union
European Convention on Human Rights **229**.1, 8, 36
    Article 8 on privacy **245**.1
European Court of Human Rights
    death penalty cases **229**.39
    margin of appreciation **229**.6
European Environment Agency (EEA) **200**.22
European Union
    AIDS strategy support **243**.29
    animal welfare legislation **233**.2
    complementary and alternative medicine research
      269.10
    elderly people
      poverty risk **239**.17, 18
      quality of life **239**.8-9
    electricity markets **204**.11-12
    energy scenarios **204**.30-31
    environmental policy **218**.7-8
    fisheries policy, ending waste discards **260**.22
    and GM crops **208**.11, 12
    herbal medicines legislation **269**.13-14, 15
    immigration decline **220**.31
    and LGBT equality **225**.11-13
    migration to UK **220**.24-5
    poverty of elderly people **239**.17, 18
    transport policies **200**.15
    waste exports **242**.18-19
    wind energy **204**.11
    UK relationship **240**.21-2
      Youth Parliament manifesto **240**.39
    and youth employment **263**.23
euthanasia **217**.1-39
    arguments against **217**.2, 3-4, 5-6, 7-8
    arguments for **217**.3, 9-10, 11-12

definitions **217**.1, 5
    doctors' opposition to **217**.22
    involuntary 5, 32
    and the law **217**.1, 24-39
    occurrence in UK **217**.24-5
    in other countries **217**.2
    of a pet **267**.9
    public attitudes to **217**.23, 34
    see also advance directives; assisted suicide;
physician assisted suicide (PAS)
eutrophication threat to ocean life **218**.24-5
EVAW (End Violence Against Women) Coalition **224**.31
evidence
    obtained under torture **229**.21-2
    secret intelligence to be allowed in court **223**.21-2
Evolve Sport **241**.35
ex-offenders
    and employment **223**.26-7
    role in cutting youth crime **223**.18
ex-service personnel **213**.31-9
    accommodation for **262**.33
    finding employment **213**.32
    homelessness **213**.35
    mental health **213**.33-4
    as mentors to young people **213**.32
    in prison **213**.4, 36, 37-9
exams
    A-levels as predictor of degree performance
      209.12; **219**.32
    and pressure on schools **209**.4
    reform **209**.6
    standards **209**.7-10
    and stress **252**.16-17
    use of smart drugs **252**.33, 34
    see also A-levels; GCSEs
executors of a will **267**.29
exercise
    children **241**.20, 35-6
      lack of exercise **241**.35
    compulsive **249**.7
    dancing, health benefits for older people **241**.
      33-4
    and depression **265**.3, 22, 24, 32, 33, 34, 38
    disabled people **255**.14-15
    fitness training tips **241**.25-6
    and health **241**.1-6, 8, 9, 32, 33-4
    lack of *see* inactivity
    low volume high-intensity training **241**.27-8
    and mental health **241**.4; **252**.26
    motivation for **241**.26, 31
    and obesity **241**.16
    Olympic legacy **241**.9, 10
    recommended amounts **241**.1, 6, 25
    running **241**.31, 32, 38-9
    and stress reduction **206**.33, 37
    and vegetarian diet **214**.29
    women's reluctance to exercise outdoors **241**.
      11-12
    Zombies, Run! fitness app **241**.38-9
    see also sport
exhaust gases *see* emissions, transport
expression, freedom of *see* freedom of expression
Extended Determinate Sentence **223**.21

extended licence period **223**.21
extinction of species **260**.2-3, 4-5
extra-marital sex and risk of heart attack **244**.33
extremism
    in schools **212**.12
    at universities **212**.13-14
Eye Movement Desensitization and Reprocessing
(EMDR) **213**.34

F

face-recognition technology and shopper
surveillance **245**.35
Facebook
    accounts, after death **267**.38
    addiction to **230**.15
    censorship of sexual content **196**.37
    children's use of **245**.25
    memorials **267**.15
    and narcissism **266**.9
    potential for data mining **245**.23-4
    and privacy **210**.33-4
    reporting inappropriate content **232**.35
    and self-esteem
    usage trends **245**.24
    see also social networking
factory farming **233**.3, 7-8
faddy eating **249**.23-4
fairness, children's rights to **229**.26
fairness complaints against broadcasters **196**.20
Fairtrade **207**.32, 33; **226**.30, 31, 36-7
    ineffectiveness **207**.33
Fairtrade Foundation **226**.27
faith *see* religion
faith-based child abuse **248**.21-3
faith healing **269**.4
faith schools **209**.22-3, 24; **215**.17-20
    and free schools programme **215**.21-2
fake alcohol **254**.13, 38
fallopian tube damage and infertility **247**.2
families **257**.1-31
    challenges **257**.6-7
    family breakdown **257**.11-12
      and children **244**.36; **257**.12-13
      and grandparents **257**.18-20
      and youth homelessness **262**.24
      see also divorce
    family structure
      changing **257**.1-2, 6, 11-12
      global variations **257**.3-5
    fatherless households **257**.11
    finances **250**.5; **257**.25-31
      child maintenance **257**.30
      childcare costs **257**.29
    and gambling **203**.33
    homeless, in B&B accommodation **262**.11
    income **257**.25-7
      and educational attainment **219**.22, 23, 25-6,
        27-8, 29-30, 34
    modern family types **257**.8-9
    right to family life **245**.1
    single-parent families **257**.11-12

    and child maintenance **257**.30-31
      worldwide **257**.3-4
    spending power falling **207**.8
    step-families **257**.21-3
    support to prevent child crime **223**.32
    see also parents; single parents; stepfamilies
Family Lives report on sexualisation of children **238**.14-15
family planning
    Millennium Development Goals **218**.39
    and population control **218**.26-7
    see also birth control; contraception
family therapy **252**.19; **249**.21
famine, effect on children **259**.26
farm produce surplus harvested for charities **242**.39
Farm to Fork programme, Tesco **271**.35-6
farming *see* agriculture
fashion industry
    and body image **234**.5-6, 11
    and fur trade **233**.19
    and living wage **229**.13
fast food
    and depression **252**.24
    litter **242**.13
fats in diet **271**.14-16
    food labelling **271**.33
    food industry fat reduction pledge **271**.13-14
    taxes on unhealthy food **241**.20-21
fatalities *see* deaths
fathers
    and childcare **221**.5
    fatherless households **257**.12
    paternity leave **221**.4-5
    teenage fathers, need for support **257**.34
fatty acids
    omega 3 **214**.29, 33
    in red meat **214**.35
Featherstone, Lynn **234**.20-21, 37
Feed-in Tariffs **204**.19, 36
feelings
    after bereavement **267**.1-4
    British reserve **267**.4-5
    after child abuse **248**.3, 4, 17, 26
    after death of a pet **267**.8-9
    depression **265**.8
    happiness **265**.38-9
fees, university *see* tuition fees, university
felt stigma, parents of disabled children **255**.26
female genital mutilation **224**.3-4, 37
femininity and dieting **234**.8
feminism and sexualisation of girls **238**.39
Ferdinand, Anton **236**.38
Ferdinand, Rio **236**.36, 38
fertility
    and abortion **231**.7
    and alcohol **254**.6
    and age **247**.2, 4, 5, 6
    problems **247**.1-3, 4
    protecting **247**.2-3, 5
    rates
      UK **257**.10
      worldwide **220**.2, 4, 9, 13, 15; **257**.3
    and smoking **261**.8
fertility drugs **247**.8-9
fertility treatments **247**.3, 7-9

and multiple births **247**.4
see also in vitro fertilisation
fetuses
  age of viability **231**.22
  fetal rights **231**.17, 18
  fetal stem cells used to treat stroke victims **211**.33
fiction about teenage suicide **258**.30
fighting animals **233**.6, 17, 27
films
  classification **196**.13-16
  depicting smoking **261**.18-19
  public opinion **196**.15-16
finance
  families **257**.25-31
  students *see* students and money matters
financial abuse **224**.1, 3
financial accounts, online, after death **267**.37
financial benefits *see* state benefits
financial concerns
  and depression **265**.2
  families **257**.25-8
  new parents **257**.28
  about older people with disabilities **255**.22-3
  of older people with HIV **243**.19
financial education **250**.17, 19, 21
financial implications of home ownership **253**.6
financial incentives for recycling waste **242**.30, 31
financial insecurity **263**.16-17
financial planning **250**.32-3
  budgeting for debt repayment **250**.37-8
  for old age **239**.14; **250**.36
  student budgeting **264**.19
  see also pensions
financial problems **250**.1, 2, 5, 32-3
  effect on health **250**.29, 33
  for separating couples **244**.33, 38-9
  and suicide risk **258**.21
  see also debt
financial sector taxes **235**.13-15
financial skills **250**.1, 2, 18
  young people **250**.17
Find and Treat service (TB) **262**.33
firearms offences **223**.5
first aid treatment
  for alcohol-related accidents **254**.17
  for drug abuse effects **228**.2
first-past-the-post electoral system **240**.29
first-time buyers **253**.4
  difficulty raising deposits **253**.1-2
  Help to Buy schemes **253**.7-8, 25
fish, in diet
  children's consumption **271**.4
  recommended intake **271**.24, 31
  vegetarian diet **214**.1
fishing industry
  environmental impact **214**.17, 25-6
  EU policy ending fish discards **260**.22
  and sustainability **218**.23
fitness
  and health **241**.1-5, 8
  lack of fitness **241**.7, 13
  obese people **241**.17
  outdoor fitness equipment **241**.36-7

Zombies, Run! fitness app **241**.38-9
  see also exercise
Fitspo (Fitspiration) **249**.29, 30
five-a-day fruit and vegetable consumption **271**.23
flags, Union Jack **240**.4-5
flexible working **263**.17-18, 33-4
  and gender equality **221**.24
flexitarian diet **214**.1
flood management **218**.6, 23
fluid intake
  during exercise **241**.26
  recommendations **271**.7, 25, 31
fly-tipping **242**.8-9, 10, 12
foetal alcohol syndrome **254**.8
foetus *see* fetuses
foil provision to heroin users **228**.26
folksonomy (social bookmarking services) **266**.1-2
food
  in the Army **213**.1
  from cloned animals **211**.10-19
    public attitudes **211**.6
    safety **211**.18, 19
  global food system **218**.29-30
  GM food *see* genetically modified (GM) food
  hunger *see* hunger
  in-vitro meat **211**.20-21
  labelling costs **207**.29
  and mental health **252**.24, 25
  natural remedies **269**.26-7
  supplies
    and climate change **216**.6-7, 10
    and factory farming **233**.8
    and GM crops **208**.19, 23-4, 32, 34-6
    and meat production **214**.5, 16
    and population growth **220**.3-4, 6
  tax on unhealthy food **241**.20-21
  UK regional specialities **240**.3
  see also diet; eating disorders; healthy eating;
meat consumption; vegetarian food
food additives **271**.10
food industry
  encouraging healthy choices **271**.6
  reducing fat content of food **271**.13-14
  and tackling childhood obesity **241**.20
food intake and overweight **241**.15-16
food labelling **271**.26
  caffeine drinks **271**.10
  date labels **242**.14, 15
  ethical labelling costs **207**.29
  GM food **208**.8
food and nutrition **271**.1-39
  see also diet; healthy eating; nutrition;
vegetarianism
food poverty in UK **235**.17; **271**.3
food production, environmental impact **214**.16, 17,
18-19, 20-21
food safety, genetically modified food **208**.2, 24
food security
  and GM crops **208**.19,23-4, 34-6
Food Standards Agency (FSA) and GM food **208**.7
food waste **242**.3, 14-16
  anaerobic digestion plant **242**.38
  by households **271**.2

restaurant doggy box scheme **242**.39
FoodSwitch app **271**.32-3
football
    and ethnic minorities **236**.12
    foreign players in the Premier League **270**.15
    match fizing **270**.33
    and racism **236**.9, 12, 13, 15, 25, 38, 39; **270**.15
force feeding of anorexia sufferer **249**.38-9
forced labour **229**.15; **227**.29-3-0
    definition **268**.39
    and human trafficking **229**.17
forced marriages **224**.3, 14-15, 36-7; **244**.3, 12-14
    action against **220**.30
    of children **248**.24-5
    and Islam **215**.12
forced migration **220**.36-7; **259**.18-23
Ford factory equal pay strike **221**.35, 36
foreign aid see aid
foreign holidays, attitudes to **222**.2
foreign nationals
    deportation and the Human Rights Act **229**.4-5
    Premier League footballers **270**.15
    prisoners **223**.25
    using NHS **251**.23, 24
forests
    and climate change **216**.11, 14-15
    conservation updates **260**.22
    destruction and tiger decline **260**.12
    dryland forests **218**.21
    rainforest protection, UN programme **218**.20-21
    restoration by introducing giant tortoises **260**.39
    see also deforestation
forums, social media **266**.1
fossil fuels **204**.6, 25
    energy industry statistics **204**.1
    subsidies **204**.4
    see also oil
fostering
    as alternative to abortion **231**.8
    foster parents' refusal to promote homosexual
lifestyle **225**.34
foundation stage education
    and character skills **219**.34-5
    and social mobility **219**.17-18
Foyer Foundation Manifesto **262**.30
Fragile X syndrome **255**.3
fragmentation mines **259**.9
France
    AIDS strategy support **243**.28
    ban on burqa wearing **215**.39
    health care **251**.9
    and sexualisation of children **238**.27-8
Francis Report (Mid-Staffs NHS Trust inquiry) **251**.3,
    4, 14-15, 16
fraud
    benefit fraud **263**.6-7
    costs of **207**.21-2
    and online information **245**.21-2
free schools **209**.19-21
    and faith schools **215**.21-2
free speech **196**.1-12
    and the Internet **230**.37, 38-9
    versus political correctness **236**.35-7
free trade **226**.13-14, 29-30, 33

and employment **226**.13-14
    negative effects **226**.13-14, 32
    and poverty **226**.14, 29-30, 33
    see also trade liberalisation
freedom of expression **196**.37
    global public opinion **229**.11-12
    and the Internet **230**.37, 38-9
    and pornography **246**.3
    versus privacy **229**.5
freedom of information **196**.38
    and the Internet **230**.37, 38-9
freedom of the press, global study **196**.1-2
freedom from surveillance **196**.38
freight transport trends **200**.22
Freshers' Week, safety on nights out **254**.35-6
freshwater resources, impact of climate change **216**.6,
10
Friends and Family Test (NHS care) **251**.33
Friends of the Earth
    opposition to non-agricultural market access **226**.15-16
    views on free trade **226**.15
fringe medicine see complementary medicine (CM)
fronto-temporal dementia **239**.28
fronto-temporal lobar degeneration (FTLD) **201**.10
fruit and vegetable consumption
    children **271**.4
    recommendations **271**.23, 31
    Victorian diet **271**.1
fruit picking jobs **263**.10-11
Fry, Stephen **258**.35
FSA (Food Standards Agency) and GM food **208**.7
FTSE 100 companies, use of tax havens **227**.35-6
fuel cells **204**.27, 38
fuel efficient homes **235**.16
fuel poverty **204**.23; **218**.3; **235**.15-16
    and microgeneration **204**.36
fundamentalism, Islamic **212**.32
funding
    AIDS strategy **243**.7, 27, 28-9
    disability benefit cuts **255**.34, 35, 38
    EMA **209**.17, 18
    faith schools **215**.17
    further education **209**.17
    higher education **209**.29, 31-2, 35
        see also tuition fees
    NHS **251**.1, 36
        funding crisis **251**.34-5, 38
        public opinions **251**.20-21
    road network **200**.6, 7, 9-10
    of social care **239**.20-23
        budget cuts **255**.24
    school sports **270**.38-9
funerals **267**.13, 30, 31-3
    green **267**.36
    paying for **267**.34-5
fungus able to break down plastic **242**.27
fur trade **233**.3-4, 18-19
further education
    barriers to take-up **263**.21-2
    funding **209**.17

G

G8 summit, climate change agreement **216**.37
Gaborone Declaration **260**.25
Galapagos penguins **260**.38-9
gambling **203**.1-39
    addiction *see* problem gambling
    definition **203**.5
    effects **203**.21-2, 28-9
    forms of **203**.4
    giving up **203**.6-7
    history of **203**.5
    online gambling **203**.28-9
        participation rates **203**.4
        women **203**.35-6
        young people **203**.17
    participation in **203**.3-4
        young people **203**.12, 16-17
    problem gamblers *see* problem gambling
    reasons for **203**.1, 9, 21, 32-3
    social context **203**.32-3
    women **203**.26, 35-6
    young people **203**.9-18
        Internet gambling **203**.16-18
        problem gambling **203**.12, 15, 16, 20
        reasons for gambling **203**.9
    see also casinos; National Lottery; problem
gambling
gamete donation *see* egg donation; sperm donation
gamete intra-fallopian transfer (GIFT) **247**.8
gaming
    and bullying **232**.25
    women **230**.2
gaming machines **203**.4
gaming platforms as social media **266**.1
Gandhi, Mohandas (Mahatma) and non-violence **259**.3
gang crime **223**.6-7, 13-15, 35-6
    and homeless young people **262**.24
Gap Action Programme, WHO **201**.36
gap years **264**.1-2
    popular destinations **222**.19
    volunteering **240**.36
Gardasil (HPV vaccine) **237**.26, 27
garlic as natural remedy **269**.27
garment industry, campaign for living wage **229**.13
gas
    green **204**.24
    natural gas industry trends **204**.1
gasification **204**.6
gastric surgery for weight loss *see* bariatric surgery
gateway drug, cannabis **256**.8, 34, 37
gay couples *see* same-sex relationships
gay marriage *see* same sex marriage
gay men
    and adoption **257**.17-18
    and ageing **239**.10-11
    awareness of gay feelings **225**.1
    and blood donation **225**.36-7
    and HIV **243**.7, 8, 21-2
    testing for STIs and HIV **243**.9
    young people, mental health problems **201**.3
    see also homosexuality
GCSEs

    ethnic minorities' performance **236**.10
    as predictor of degree results **219**.32
    reform **209**.6
GDP (Gross Domestic Product) as poor measure of
living standards **226**.14
gender **221**.1, 11
    and attitudes to higher education **209**.27
    and attitudes to school **209**.11
    and cannabis use **256**.15
    and colour preferences **221**.7-8
    and compulsive shopping **207**.6
    and education *see* gender and education
    and employment **221**.1-2, 18, 19, 27-9, 37
        see also women in the workforce
    and gambling **203**.16
    and health issues **252**.9-10
    and HIV sufferers in UK **243**.14
    and household tasks **221**.6
    and Internet usage **230**.2-4
    and media usage **210**.12
    and the news **210**.6-8
    and pay *see* gender pay gap
    and sport participation **270**.3
    and work **221**.27-9
    see also gender pay gap; men; women
gender abortions **231**.18, 30-31
gender assignation **225**.8
gender-based violence *see* domestic abuse; rape
gender dysphoria **225**.20, 21-2
gender and education
    attitudes to school **209**.11
    higher education **209**.27
gender equality
    in families **257**.7
    international initiatives **221**.2
    and Islam **215**.12
    legal rights **221**.2, 3
    and school uniforms **268**.16
Gender Equality Duty (GED) **225**.7
gender identity disorder **225**.20
gender inequality **221**.1-2, 33-5, 37
    at work **221**.1-2, 18, 19, 27, 37
    definition **221**.11
    worldwide **221**.1-2, 33-9
gender pay gap **221**.22-5, 27-8, 35-6, 37
Gender Recognition Act 2004 **225**.6, 20, 27
gender quotas, company boards **221**.16, 21
gender segregation in university talks **264**.21-2
gender stereotyping **221**.11, 33
    children **238**.3, 14, 33-4
    and employment **221**.23, 28, 29
    and sexualisation **238**.3, 14
    and toys **221**.7-8; **238**.33-4
genderqueer **225**.20
gene mapping **208**.13
gene splicing *see* genetic modification
gene therapy as cure for HIV **243**.32, 33
general practitioners *see* GPs (general practitioners)
general anxiety disorder (GAD) **206**.11, 14-15;
  265.17
Generation Y Not entrepreneurs **264**.10-11
genes
    and anxiety **206**.3

and divorce **244**.32
and eating disorders **249**.5
and gambling addiction **203**.30-31
human genes implanted into animals **233**.39
and lifespan **239**.2
and mental health **201**.33
and obesity **241**.16
and sexual orientation **225**.1-2
and stress **206**.30-31
genetic diseases
and sex selection **247**.35
testing of embryos **247**.8
and three-parent IVF **247**.29-34
genetic modification
applications **208**.6, 19-22, 37-8
arguments against **208**.3-4, 5, 17
arguments for **208**.2, 3, 17
definition **208**.1, 3
and the environment **208**.20, 22, 29
generations of plants **208**.1-2
human cells transplated into animals **233**.39
method **208**.14
risks **208**.17
testing **208**.1
see also genetically modified animals; genetically
modified crops; genetically modified food
genetic testing of embryos **247**.8
genetically modified (GM) animals **208**.3, 13-14, 37-9
chickens **208**.14, 37-8
experiments on **208**.37-8
fish **214**.25-6
salmon **208**.31, 39
genetically modified (GM) crops **208**.1-2
and animal feed **208**.8, 24
arguments for and against **208**.5, 9-10, 17, 34
cross-contamination **208**.24, 26
developing countries **208**.10
and food supply **208**.19, 23-4, 32, 34-6
risks **208**.27-8
UK **208**.5, 17-18
genetically modified (GM) food **208**.5-8
arguments against **208**.23-4, 31-2
effects on health **208**.5, 8, 19-20
public attitudes to **208**.18, 29-30; **211**.6
safety **208**.1, 2, 7
Geneva Conventions **259**.7, 28
and child soldiers **268**.25
genital herpes **237**.20
genital warts **237**.20
genocide **259**.27-8
geospatial tagging **266**.2
geothermal energy **204**.3, 27
Germany
AIDS strategy support **243**.28
health care **251**.9
privacy rights **245**.4
Ghana
impact of free trade **226**.29, 32
income growth **235**.30
withdrawal of aid due to anti-gay laws **225**.14
ghost tourism **222**.16
giant tortoises and forest restoration **260**.39
Gibson inquiry into use of torture **229**.22, 23
Gilderdale, Kay **217**.27-8, 29, 34

ginger as natural remedy **269**.27
ginger bullying **232**.16
Ginkgo biloba extract and dementia treatment **269**.22
Girlguiding UK
body confidence campaign **234**.34
survey on media pressure on girls **238**.13
girls and young women
attitudes to school **209**.11
and beauty pageants **238**.28-30
and body image **234**.9, 25-6, 31
child soldiers **259**.24
and cosmetic surgery **234**.33, 34
and education **221**.31-2, 35, 38-9
and ending child marriage **268**.29-30
effect on population control **220**.7
programmes in developing countries **229**.27-8
HPV vaccination **237**.27, 28, 29-31
media influences **238**.3, 13
and parental separation **244**.36
and prostitution **246**.27-8, 34-8
and school PE **270**.23
and sexual violence **238**.17
sexualisation of **221**.9-10; 8-9, 27-39
single-sex education **221**.31-2
toy preferences **221**.7-8
violence against **224**.28-31
girls' schools **221**.31-2
Girls' Union **246**.21
Give Yourself a Chance campaign **234**.34
glamping **222**.20
glass ceiling **221**.21-2
Gleaning Network UK **242**.39
global alcohol consumption guidelines **254**.18
global development delay **255**.3
Global Emergency Overview app **266**.34
global financial crisis **235**.13-14
Global Media Monitoring Project **210**.6-8
global poverty **235**.23-39
statistics **235**.23, 24
global targets on child protection **248**.32-3
Global Tiger Recovery Program (GTRP) **269**.17
global trade **226**.26-39
global warming **216**.8, 9; **218**.19
measurement **216**.26-7
see also climate change; energy efficiency;
greenhouse gas emissions
globalisation **226**.1-25
definition **226**.1, 13
effects of **226**.2, 13, 20-21, 24-5
and ethical consumerism **207**.23
need for international cooperation **226**.17-19, 21, 22-5
and trade **226**.26-39
GM crops see genetically modified (GM) crops
gonorrhoea **237**.20-21, 24-5
Good Times app **254**.36
Goodger, Lauren **234**.6-7
Goody, Jade, and cervical cancer screening **237**.32
Google
censorship requests from governments **196**.29
data requests from governments **245**.13
Google Circles **245**.3
Street View **210**.33; **245**.38-9
withdrawal from China **196**.27-8, 29, 30
Gosling, Ray **217**.29

gossip magazines and eating disorders **249**.28
gourmand syndrome **249**.8
government, UK **240**.3, 21, 26
    body confidence campaign **234**.20-21, 37, 39
    control of broadcasters **196**.18-19
    devolved government **240**.27-8
    domestic violence definitions **224**.34-7
    ethnic minority members **236**.11
    government ministers **240**.26
    healthy behaviour promotion **234**.11-12
    and the monarchy **240**.22
    open data policies **245**.12-13
    and religion **215**.6
    women's representation **221**.13, 15, 20, 37
    see also Parliament
government policies
    on alcohol **254**.19-20
        minimum unit pricing **254**.14, 19, 37-8
    benefit reform **263**.9
    child poverty strategy **235**.19
    on crime **223**.23-5
        gang crime **223**.13-15
    on drugs **228**.24-7
        see also classification of drugs
    on education **209**.17, 18, 19, 24
        academies **209**.25, 26
    employment support for disabled people **255**.31, 32-3
    and financial pressures **250**.32
    on genetically modified crops **208**.5
    on home ownership **253**.7-8, 9, 25
    on homelessness **262**.8-9
    on house building **253**.24
    on Internet porn regulation **246**.15-16
    on mental health **201**.5
    and obesity **271**.6-7, 9
    on preventing violence against women and girls
224.28-31
    on prostitution **246**.17-18
    on public health **219**.13
    renewable energy **204**.4, 7-8, 15-16
    school sports funding **270**.38-9
    sensible drinking guidelines *see* daily benchmarks
on alcohol consumption
    on social mobility **219**.17-21
    on unemployment **263**.3
    waste management **242**.1-4, 9
    welfare reforms **235**.9, 10
governments
    control of the Internet **196**.32-5
    data requests to Google **245**.13
    Internet censorship requests **196**.29
GPs (general practitioners)
    and anxiety sufferers **252**.15
    and depression treatment **265**.3-4
    and eating disorders **249**.21, 33
    and obesity management **271**.6-7
    and young people **252**.5
    see also doctors
graduates
    destinations **264**.39
    earnings **264**.11
    employment **264**.32-4
    internships **264**.36-7

    job searches **263**.24-5; **264**.35, 37
    starting salaries **263**.25
graffiti, racist **236**.14
grandparents, contact after family breakdown **257**.18-20
Grannynet website **239**.38
grants, student **250**.24
grapes as natural remedy **269**.27
Great Ocean Conveyor **216**.8
Great Pacific Garbage Patch **242**.21
GREATDREAM keys to happier living **265**.38-9
greater horseshoe bat **260**.1
Greece
    housework gender division **263**.15
    smoking ban **261**.31
green belt land threats **253**.38-9
green cars *see* fuel efficient cars
green funerals **267**.36
green gas **204**.24
green spaces, mental health benefits **265**.35
Green Tobacco Sickness **261**.9
green tourism *see* ecotourism; responsible travel;
sustainable tourism
greenhouse effect **216**.1
greenhouse gases
    emission reduction targets **216**.7, 33
    emission trends **216**.7
    emissions
        from livestock farming **214**.17, 18, 19, 21
        from transport **200**.14, 15, 22
        from waste incineration **242**.34-5
    and GM crops **208**.22
    see also carbon dioxide emissions
Greenhouse project **253**.37
greening out **256**.9
Greenland ice sheet **216**.15
greenwashing **222**.24
grey long-eared bats **260**.7
grief **267**.1-4
    animals **267**.10
    and depression **239**.32; **267**.4
    getting help **267**.3, 4, 6-7
    healing from **267**.7
    prolonged (complicated) **267**.3-4, 6-7
    stages of **267**.1-2
    symptoms **267**.2
Griffin, Nick **236**.37
Groan Ups **257**.9
grocery shopping, online **207**.10
grooming **246**.34, 35-6; **248**.30, 31
    online **230**.23-4
Gross Domestic Product (GDP) as poor measure of
living standards **226**.14
ground source heat pumps **204**.35
growth hormones, risks **270**.32
Guantánamo Bay **212**.33-5
    torture of detainees **212**.36-7
guided busways **200**.30, 32
Guiding Principles on Business and Human Rights
(UN) **227**.27, 28
guilt
    and grief **267**.2
    at loss of a pet **267**.8
    and pornography use **246**.2

and post traumatic stress disorder **201**.21
gun crime **223**.5
Guru Nanak and non-violence **259**.4
gutkha (chewing tobacco) **261**.10
Gypsies and Travellers, discrimination against **236**.21-2
    Scotland **236**.22

H

HAART *see* antiretroviral therapy
habitat loss
    tigers **260**.12
    see also deforestation
Hague Conventions **259**.7-8
Haiti
    debt and disater **226**.6
    relief workers bringing cholera **259**.29-30
Halal slaughter **233**.16
halls of residence **209**.30
hallucinogens (psychedelics) **228**.3-4, 14
hangovers **254**.3-4
happiness
    declining, children and young people **258**.29
    GREATDREAM keys to happier living **265**.38-9
    and health, teenagers **241**.8
    and marriage **244**.10
harassment
    definition **221**.3; **225**.28
    by journalists, Editor' Code **210**.28
    racial **236**.1-2
    on sexual orientation grounds **225**.28
    in sport **270**.9
hard-to-reach children and education **268**.22, 23
hate crime
    against disabled people **255**.11
    anti-Muslim **215**.28-30; **236**.14, 24
        see also Islamophobia
    homophobic **225**.29, 30-31, 32
hazardous waste **218**.12
    EU trade **242**.18-19
    illegal dumping **242**.10-11
HDTV **210**.11, 14
head injuries in sport **270**.36
headaches and acupuncture treatment **269**.2
headteachers, concern about extremism in schools
    212.12
health **252**.1-39
    and alcohol **254**.1, 3-4, 5-6, 7, 8
        fake alcohol **254**.13
    and anxiety **206**.10
    and body image **234**.10, 11
    and cannabis
        benefits **256**.19, 20
        risks **256**.8, 9, 11-13, 17, 21, 32
    and car travel **200**.1, 23
    children's rights **229**.24
    and climate change **216**.7, 10
    and divorce **244**.33
    and drug abuse **228**.12-13
    and fat consumption **271**.14, 15-16, 22
    and fuel poverty **235**.15-16
    and GM crops **208**.19-20, 29

HIV sufferers **243**.18, 30-31
    and homelessness **262**.6, 20-21, 26-7, 32-3
    inequalities **235**.6-7
        global **268**.20
        UK **268**.18
    and marriage **244**.10
        child marriage **244**.15; **268**.28-9
    and meat consumption **214**.16, 34-5
    and money worries **250**.29, 33
    and obesity **241**.15, 17; **271**.9, 20
    older people **239**.3-4, 8, 27
        depression **239**.31-2
        health problems **239**.4, 24-6
        lesbian, gay and bisexual people **239**.10
        see also dementia
    and physical activity **241**.1-5, 9, 32, 33-4
        disabled people **255**.14-15
    and population growth **220**.2
    risks for sports players **270**.8, 36-8
    and salt intake **271**.12
    and sleep **264**.24
    and smoking **261**.1, 2-3, 4, 8-9, 10
        benefits of giving up **261**.9, 17, 21
        passive smoking **261**.14
    and social class **219**.11-13
    and sugar consumption **271**.18-19, 21
    travel health advice **222**.10
    and vegetarian diets **214**.4-5, 9, 12, 28-33, 36-9
    and waste incinerators **242**.36
    see also mental health; mental illness; sexual health
health care **251**.1-39
    clinics in schools, Youth Parliament manifesto **240**.38
    NHS *see* NHS
    restricting treatment of smokers and obese
people **261**.22-3
    sources of advice for young people **252**.4-5
    see also care services for older people
Health Check programme **251**.3
Health and Safety at Work Act and stress **206**.25,
28
health service *see* National Health Service
Health and Social Care Act **251**.3-4, 25-6, 29
health tourists **251**.23
health warnings on cigarette packs **261**.27
Health and Well-being Boards **251**.26, 31
Healthwatch **251**.26, 31-2
healthy eating **271**.23-5
    advice linked to eating disorders **249**.21
    and ageing **239**.27
    on a budget **271**.31
    eatwell plate **271**.39
    FoodSwitch app **271**.32-3
    and meat consumption **214**.34-5
    and mental health **252**.25
    and schools **252**.30; **271**.6, 34
    and stress **206**.33
    and vegetarian diets **214**.28-30, 33, 36, 37, 38-9
    see also diet; food and nutrition
Healthy magazine, airbrushing **234**.27-8
Healthy Lives, Healthy People Government strategy
    219.13; **271**.9
healthy weight maintenance *see* weight
management
hearing loss, older people **239**.25

heart
    effects of alcohol **254**.3, 5
    effects of smoking **261**.1, 4, 8
heart attack risk of men having affairs **244**.33
heart disease **239**.25
    and animal research **233**.35-6
    as cause of death **267**.20
    and red meat consumption **214**.35
    and stress **206**.4
    and vegetarian diet **214**.31-2
heart transplant, Britain's first **251**.2
heat pumps, microgeneration **204**.35
Heavily Indebted Poor Countries (HIPC) initiative **226**.5-6
heavy drinking *see* alcohol abuse
Help to Buy schemes **253**.25
hens
    battery farmed **233**.3, 7
    genetically modified **208**.14, 37-8
hepatitis B **237**.21
herbal medicines **269**.4
    and dementia treatment **269**.21-2
    and depression treatment
    regulation **269**.4, 13-14, 15
    phobia treatment **206**.13
heredity *see* genes
heroin, signs of use **228**.14-15
herpes, genital **237**.20
HGH (human growth hormones), risks **270**.32
hidden child abuse **248**.8
hidden children (migrants) **268**.36-7
hidden disabilities **255**.41
    and public attitudes **255**.28, 37
hidden homelessness **262**.1-2
high blood pressure (hypertension) **241**.4
    and cannabis use **256**.8
    and salt intake **271**.12
high earners, attitudes to pay **227**.24-5
high-intensity training **241**.27-8
high-speed rail **200**.35, 36, 37-9
higher apprenticeships **264**.2, 3, 6
higher education **209**.27-39
    alternative options **264**.1-2, 3, 29
    black students, employment prospects **236**.19-20
    business partnerships **264**.6
    costs and benefits **264**.11
    degree results and school background **209**.12
    disability rights **255**.29-30
    and ethnic minorities **236**.10
    funding **209**.2, 31-2, 35; **250**.22-5
    parental encouragement **209**.36
    reasons for not participating **209**.27, 28; **264**.12
    record number of applications **209**.37-8
    and social class **209**.34-5
    social media and student engagement **266**.30-31
    student life **209**.30-33; **264**.14-31
    value of **264**.11
    young people's attitudes to **209**.27-8
    see also further education; graduates; students;
    universities
highly active antiretroviral therapy *see* antiretroviral
therapy
hijab ban on basketball player **270**.24-5
Hinduism **215**.2
    and abortion **231**.19
    and faith schools **215**.21
    and pornography **246**.1
    and vegetarianism **214**.6
    and war and peace **259**.3
historic child abuse **248**.36
HIV (Human Immunodeficiency Virus) **237**.21; **243**.1-39
    cure **243**.32-5, 37-9
    definition **243**.1
    and discrimination **243**.15-17
    education **243**.10-11
    effects **243**.2
    infection rate
        UK **243**.5
        worldwide **243**.6, 26-7
    living with HIV **243**.14-25
        children **243**.23-5
        older people 19-20, 30-31
    prevalence **243**.2
    and quality of life **243**.18-19
    risk groups **243**.6-7, 8-9
    symptoms **243**.2
    testing for **243**.3, 9, 35, 36
    timeline **243**.7
    transmission **243**.1-2
        criminalisation **243**.11
        mother-to-child **243**.1-2, 25
    treatments **243**.3-4
        worldwide access **243**.6
    UK statistics **243**.2, 5, 14-15
    worldwide statistics **243**.6-7
    and young people **243**.23-5
    see also AIDS
holidays
    Army leave **213**.2
    attitudes to **222**.2
    costs **222**.5, 6-7
    destinations
        Britain as holiday destination **222**.2-3, 5, 11
        gap year travel **222**.19
        reasons for choice **222**.2-3, 11
        trends **222**.1
    see also responsible tourism; tourism
holistic therapies **269**.11
Holy War **259**.3, 5
home building **253**.16
    affordable homes **253**.28
    council targets reduced **253**.27
    funded by councils selling high-value properties **253**.29-30
    on green belt **253**.38-9
    terraced houses **253**.31
home care services and older people's human
rights **229**.33-4
home environments
    and cannabis use by young people **256**.6
    and educational attainment **219**.27, 33
home ownership
    difficulties for young people **253**.2-3, 5
    Help to Buy schemes **253**.6, 7-8, 9, 25
    pros and cons **253**.6
    trends **253**.3
Home Ownership for People with Long-Term

Disabilities (HOLD) **253**.8
home security and students **264**.17
home testing for HIV **243**.36
homelessness **262**.1-39
    accommodation for homeless people **262**.7, 9, 31, 33
    attitudes to **262**.12, 14-15, 16, 17
    causes **262**.1, 4, 5, 24
    and children **262**.6
    criminalisation of **262**.18
    definitions **262**.1
    effects **262**.6, 20, 32-3
    ex-service personnel **213**.35
    experience of **262**.25
    and health **262**.6, 20-21, 26-7, 32-3
    help for homeless people **262**.8-9, 31-9
    hidden homeless **262**.1-2
    history of **262**.8-9
    local authority responsibilities **262**.3, 9
    and mental health **262**.2, 14, 19
    priority needs groups **262**.3
    rough sleeping **262**.6, 9, 32, 36
      support services **262**.36-7, 38
    statistics **253**.23; **262**.1, 32
    stereotypes and misconceptions **262**.14-15
    young people **262**.22-30
      reasons for homelessness **262**.15, 24
    see also street homelessness; temporary
accommodation
homeopathy **269**.1-2
    and the NHS **269**.34-5, 36
    public opinions **269**.32-3
    regulation **269**.12
    and seasonal affective disorder **265**.11
homesickness, students **264**.16
homestays (holidays) **222**.24
homicide crimes **223**.4-5
homophobia
    homophobic bullying **225**.9, 29; **232**.12-13
      and schools **225**.7, 8
    prevention strategies **232**.15
homophobic crime **225**.29, 30-31, 32
homosexuality **225**.1-4
    causes **225**.1-2, 15-16
    'curing' **225**.2, 16, 17-18
    and human rights **229**.31-2
    self-awareness of **225**.1
    see also gay men; lesbians; LGBT people; same-
sex relationships
honey as natural remedy **269**.27
honour based violence **224**.3
hookah smoke (shisha) **261**.2, 3, 10
hormones and ageing **239**.1
horses
    fighting **233**.27
    Przewalski's horse conservation **233**.26
hospices **267**.15, 25
Hospital Plan (1962) **251**.2
hospitals
    A&E waiting times **251**.17
    admissions under Mental Health Act **201**.38
    alcohol-related admissions **254**.14
    Britons hospitalized overseas **222**.15
    care standards **251**.8
    elderly patients **251**.11-13
    Friends and Family test **251**.33
Hostels Capital Improvement Programme (HCIP)
    262.9
hotel industry
    eco-lodges **222**.24
    and ethics **222**.31-2
hours of work *see* working hours
House of Lords, and bishops **215**.6
household debt **250**.5, 11
household waste **218**.11, 12; **242**.22
    food waste **242**.14-16
    government policies **242**.3-4
    incineration **242**.34-6
    recycling **242**.23-4, 30, 31
    see also composting waste; waste management
households
    gender roles **221**.6
    low-income **235**.5-8
    minimum standard income **235**.5
    spending **207**.7
    spending power falling **207**.8
    see also families; homeless households
housework
    and gender **221**.6; **263**.15
    housework sharing and risk of divorce **244**.32
housing **253**.1-39
    benefits **263**.9
    building *see* home building
    and climate change **216**.29-30
    empty homes **253**.18, 32-5
    energy efficient **235**.16
    home design and privacy **245**.2
    immigrants and social housing **220**.28, 29
    people with learning disabilities **255**.13-14
    policies **253**.18, 24, 25-6
    and poverty **235**.7
    priority needs households **262**.3
    problems for separating couples **244**.38-9
    problems for mental health sufferers **201**.29
    rent scams warning for students **264**.18
    rented sector **253**.1, 10-13
    shortage **253**.16, 19-20, 23
    social housing *see* social housing
    sustainable **253**.36, 37
    see also affordable housing; home ownership;
homelessness; rural housing; temporary accommodation
Housing Act 1996 **262**.3
housing benefits cuts and youth homelessness **262**.29
How Good is Porn campaign **246**.6
How to Look Good Naked (TV programme) **234**.19
HPV (human papilloma virus) **237**.20, 26
    and cancer **237**.26
    vaccination programme **251**.3
    vaccines **237**.26-7, 28, 29-31
human cloning **211**.22-39
    arguments for and against **211**.26-7
    ethical issues **211**.8-9, 26-7
    legislation **211**.25
    therapeutic cloning **211**.9, 22-3
human embryos *see* embryos
Human Fertilisation and Embryology Bill **211**.25; **231**.2
human growth hormones (HGHs), risks **270**.32
human immunodeficiency virus *see* HIV

human reproductive cloning **211**.22, 24-7
Human Reproductive Cloning Act **211**.25
human rights **229**.1-23
    and business **227**.27-8
    children *see* children's rights
    definition **229**.1
    and Internet access **230**.38-9
    public attitudes to **229**.11-12
    water and sanitation **218**.32
Human Rights Act **229**.1-8
    arguments against **229**.7-8
    arguments for **229**.8
    coverage **229**.1-2
    and freedom of expression **196**.14
    fundamental rights and freedoms **229**.2
    and home care **229**.34
    myths **229**.3-6
    rights to private and family life **245**.1
    and sexual orientation **225**.7
Human Rights Risk Atlas **229**.9
human trafficking *see* trafficking
humanism **215**.4
    and euthanasia **217**.6
    and war and peace **259**.5
humanitarian aid workers, mobile apps **266**.34
humanitarian intervention **259**.29-30
Humanitarian Kiosk app **266**.34
Hungarian immigrants **236**.32
hunger
    children, worldwide **259**.26
    food poverty, UK **235**.17
    impact of biofuels **204**.33-4
    Millennium Development Goals **235**.26-7
    worldwide **220**.6
hunting lions **260**.29, 30-31
hybridization **211**.2
    see also cross-contamination
hydration **271**.7, 25, 31
hydro power **204**.19, 27
hydrogen power **204**.26-7, 38
hydrogenated (trans) fat **271**.15
hypermasculinity **238**.17
hypertension *see* high blood pressure
hypnosis **269**.4
hypnotherapy **252**.15

I

IBRD (International Bank for Reconstruction and Development) **226**.10
ice sheets, impact of climate change **216**.12, 15
ICT
    education **230**.13
    see also computers; Internet
IDA (International Development Association) **226**.9
identity
    British *see* British identity
    national, impact of globalization **226**.12
identity fraud **207**.19-20; **230**.24
    young people's risk of **245**.21-2
IFAW investigation of online wildlife trade **260**.17-18

iGDACS app **266**.34
Ile aux Aigrettes, giant tortoise reintroduction **260**.39
illegal abortion **231**.12
illegal dumping *see* fly-tipping
illegal wildlife trade **260**.16-26
Illegal Wildlife Trade Conference, speech by Prince Charles **260**.18-20
illness and malnutrition **271**.5
ILO *see* International Labour Organisation
IMF *see* International Monetary Fund
imitation as indirect racism **236**.28
immigration
    attitudes to **220**.22-3, 26, 27-8
    David Cameron's speech **220**.30-31
    and domestic violence victims **224**.37
    European Union **220**.31
    immigrants' use of NHS **251**.23, 24
    integration of immigrants **240**.15-16, 19
    and population diversity **240**.15
    and social housing **220**.28, 29
    UK **220**.21-2, 24-5
    see also asylum seekers; ethnic minorities; migrant workers; migration
immune system and fertility **247**.8
implants, contraceptive **237**.7
import tariffs **226**.26-7
importation of indecent articles **196**.23
imprisonment *see* prison
in-law relationships and risk of divorce **244**.32
in vitro fertilization (IVF) **247**.7, 9-10
    and acupuncture **269**.2
    experience of **247**.11-12
    numbers of babies born **247**.13; **257**.10
    and older women **247**.22-6
    and same-sex couples **247**.27
    sex offender's right to IVF **247**.28
    three-parent IVF to prevent genetic diseases **247**.29-34
    using unused embryos for research **211**.31
in vitro maturation **247**.8
in vitro meat **211**.20-21
inactivity **241**.1, 7, 16; **271**.8
    children **241**.35
    health risks **241**.1-2
inappropriate relationships and sexual exploitation **268**.35-6
incapacity benefits **263**.9
incentives for recycling **242**.31
incineration of waste **242**.34-6
    plant threatening waste pickers' jobs, India **242**.29
    to produce energy **242**.32-3
    Sweden importing waste for energy plants **242**.37
inclusion and sport **270**.12-25
Income Tax **250**.13
incomes
    and children's educational attainment **219**.22, 23, 25-6, 27-8, 29-30, 34
    family incomes **257**.25, 26-7
    high earners' attitudes to pay **227**.24-5
    income calculation for debt repayment **250**.37
    income shocks and child labour **268**.4
    inequalities **219**.8, 16; **227**.15, 16
        and Internet access **230**.4, 5

see also rich-poor gap
low-income households **235**.5-8
middle classes **219**.2, 3, 9-10
minimum standard **235**.3, 5
minimum wage **263**.5-6
perceptions of wage levels **219**.15
see also earnings; gender pay gap; salaries; wages
indecency offences **196**.22-3
indecent images **248**.10-11
independence
disabled people **255**.1
Scotland **240**.5, 6, 32
Independent Living Fund **255**.35, 38, 41
independent shops **207**.28
threat from supermarkets **207**.26, 27
indeterminate sentences **223**.20
India
censorship of sexual content on the Internet **196**.37
child labour **268**.5-6, 7-9
as gap year destination **222**.19
gender inequality **221**.1
impact of free trade **226**.30
plastic bags used in road surfacing **242**.28
privacy rights **245**.4
surrogate mothers and health risks **247**.20-21
waste pickers threatened by incinerator plant **242**.29
indicator species **260**.38
indigenous people
Amazon town ban on tourists **222**.32
impact of tourism **222**.21-3, 29-30, 33-4
indirect discrimination
against Gypsies and Travellers **236**.22
racial **236**.2
and sexual orientation **225**.28
indirect euthanasia (doctrine of double effect) **217**.5, 14
indirect racism **236**.28
Indonesia
child soldiers **268**.24
children and smoking **261**.38-9
palm oil industry and tiger decline **260**.12
inequality
in distribution of work **263**.39
and the environment **218**.3-4
gender *see* gender inequality
health **219**.11-13
of incomes **219**.8, 16
schools admissions **219**.24
and social mobility **219**.16
UK **235**.12, 13
wealth inequalities, effects and policy suggestions **263**.12
see also child poverty; poverty; rich-poor gap
Infant Life Preservation Act 1929 **231**.1
infant mortality and child marriage **268**.29
infection-triggered auto immune anorexia nervosa **249**.7-8
infertility **247**.1-3, 4
see also fertility; fertility treatments
information
evaluating online information **230**.10-12
online searching and gender **230**.3
personal, control of **230**.24, 30; **245**.11-27

security of information and social networking **210**.30-31
see also Freedom of Information Act
information technology (IT)
impact on work **263**.38
see also computers; Internet
Inglis, Frances **217**.27, 29
inhaling alcohol **254**.33-4
inherited wealth **219**.8
injections, contraceptive **237**.7
injured service personnel **213**.2, 7, 8-9, 10-11
injuries, sports
head injuries **270**.36
insurance against **270**.8-9
psychological effects **270**.37-8
innovations of the decade **210**.17-18
insects
bees, environmental update **260**.22
butterfly populations decline **260**.21
effect of GM crops **208**.27
insecurity
financial **263**.16-17
job insecurity and stress **263**.31
instant messaging (IM) **266**.2
and bullying **232**.25
reporting misuse **232**.36
support for anxiety sufferers **252**.14-15
insulin **271**.21
and biotechnology **211**.3
insurance industry
and climate change studies **216**.18-19
discrimination against mental health sufferers **265**.7
integrated healthcare **269**.7
integration
British Muslims **240**.17-18
immigrants **236**.17; **240**.15-16, 19
into society **215**.9
racial *see* racial integration
intellectual impairment and cannabis use **256**.22-4
intellectual property rights *see* patents
intensive farming **233**.3, 7-8
interfaith relations, public attitudes to **212**.30-31
Intergovernmental Panel on Climate Change (IPCC) **216**.3, 5, 37
criticism of reports **216**.22-3
internal climate variability **216**.1
internal conflicts **259**.1
internalised stigma about HIV **243**.17
internally displaced persons **259**.18-19, 23
Syria **259**.20
International Bank for Reconstruction and Development (IBRD) **226**.10
International Centre for Settlement of Investment Disputes (ICSID) **226**.10
international companies *see* multinational corporations
International Criminal Court **259**.2, 8, 28
International Day of the Girl **248**.24
International Development Association (IDA) **226**.9
International Finance Corporation (IFC) **226**.10
International Fund for Anmal Welfare (IFAW) study of online wildlife trade **260**.17-18
international humanitarian law **259**.1, 7-8
and child soldiers **268**.25
International Labour Organisation (ILO) **229**.14

and child labour **268**.2, 25
and child soldiers **268**.25
international labour standards **229**.14-16
international laws and child soldiers **268**.24-6
international migration *see* migration
International Monetary Fund (IMF) **226**.11-12
and aid **235**.32
International Security Assistance Force (ISAF) in
Afghanistan **259**.32
international trade **226**.26-39
and poverty **226**.28, 29-30, 33
UK initiatives **226**.28
see also free trade; globalization
International Union for the Conservation of Nature
and Natural Resources (IUCN) Red List **260**.1, 5, 22
international unity, need for **226**.18-19
International Women's Day **221**.36
Internet
access by children **238**.3
access devices **210**.11, 13
addiction **230**.14, 16-17, 18; **266**.13
advertising **230**.5
junk food **271**.28, 29-30
broadband access **230**.6-8
bullying *see* cyberbullying
and censorship **196**.27-39
Australia **196**.30
China **196**.27-8, 30
government censorship requests **196**.29
Iran **196**.32, 33
outsourcing **196**.33-4
sexual content **196**.36-8
UK **196**.31
and child sex abuse **196**.39; **248**.29
and consumer power **207**.4
cookies **245**.9-10
friendships **265**.18
gambling *see* online gambling
and homeless people **262**.34-5
as a human right **230**.38-9
and innovations of the decade **210**.17
and junk food advertising **271**.28, 29-30
network filters **238**.16, 25, 26; **246**.7, 15-16
news, and women **210**.8
and newspapers **210**.19
online activity **230**.1-5
children **230**.4-5; **238**.3; **245**.25-7
and gender **230**.2-4
older people **230**.5
young people **230**.4-5, 8-9, 33
online bullying *see* cyberbullying
online safety **248**.10-11
parental controls **238**.5, 25; **245**.26-7
pornography **246**.3
children viewing **196**.38; **238**.3-4, 16, 19;
246.10-11
filters to block pornography **238**.16, 25, 26;
246.7, 15-16
and the law **246**.7-8
petition against **238**.26
and privacy **245**.3, 16-27
pro-eating disorder websites **249**.29-31
removing online content **232**.35, 36

safety *see* safety and the Internet
sexting **238**.23-4
shopping
consumer rights **207**.13
and gender **230**.2, 3-4
grocery shopping **207**.10
international comparisons **210**.15
safety **207**.10
trade in protected wildlife and ivory **260**.17-18, 20
and travel booking **222**.3
trends **210**.5
trolls **232**.32, 37; **266**.14, 15
usage trends **230**.1-5
see also child pornography; e-mail; safety and the
Internet; social networking; websites
see also under online
Internet Service Providers (ISPs) code of practice
246.15
Internet Service Providers Association (ISPA)
criticism of Communications Data Bill **245**.6
Internet Watch Foundation (IWF) **196**.31, 37; **246**.8
sexual abuse survey **248**.29
internships **219**.20, 37-8; **264**.36-7
interpersonal therapy **252**.19; **265**.24, 26
intersex **225**.20
intestacy **267**.29
intestines, effects of alcohol **254**.6
intra-cytoplasmic sperm injection (ICSI) **247**.7
Inuit and seal hunting **233**.22
investment and human rights concerns **229**.9-10
involuntary euthanasia **217**.5
Belgium **217**.32
involuntary smoking *see* passive smoking
iPads and accessing newspaper content **210**.19
IPCC *see* Intergovernmental Panel on Climate
Change
iPS cells (induced pluripotent stem cells) **211**.35-7
IQ and likelihood of drug abuse **228**.11
Iran
arms deals with Britain **259**.11
death penalty **229**.37
demonstrations via the Internet **196**.32
government control of the Internet **196**.33
Iraq
conflict **259**.1-2
weapons supplied by UK **259**.11
women's rights following US invasion **259**.34
Ireland
cannabis laws **256**.28
HIV incidence **243**.35
mandatory reporting of chid abuse **248**.37
plastic bag charge **242**.25
smoking ban **261**.31
see also Northern Ireland
iron in the diet
red meat **214**.34
and vegetarian diet **214**.29, 30, 33
Islam **215**.2-3; 9-12
and abortion **231**.19
and gender equality **215**.12
and marriage **215**.12
and pornography **246**.1
public perceptions of **212**.4, 30-31

Sharia law **215**.11-12
    and terrorism **212**.8-10, 32; **215**.10-11
    and war and peace **259**.5
    see also Muslims
Islamophobia **215**.30. 31-2
    and the media **215**.33; **236**.23-4
    in schools **236**.15
island nations, impacts of climate change **216**.16-17; **220**.38
isolation
    as abuse **224**.1
    mental health sufferers **201**.6
    see also loneliness
ISPA (Internet Service Providers Association) criticism of Communications Data Bill **245**.6
IT *see* information technology
Italy
    AIDS strategy support **243**.29
    smoking ban **261**.31
IUCN (International Union for the Conservation of Nature and Natural Resources) Red List **260**.1, 5, 22
IVF *see* in vitro fertilization
Ivory Coast, use of drones **259**.13
ivory trade
    online trade **260**.17, 20
    and poaching **260**.9-11, 24-5
IWF (Internet Watch Foundation) **196**.31, 37

J

jail *see* prison
Jamaica, cannabis laws **256**.29
James, Daniel (assisted suicide case) **217**.21
Japan, AIDS strategy support **243**.28
Jehovah's Witnesses and abortion **231**.19
Jersey, abortion law **231**.3
Jews (Judaism) **215**.3
    and abortion **231**.19
    anti-semitism **215**.36
    and faith schools **215**.21-2
    religious slaughter **233**.16
    and vegetarianism **214**.6
jihad **212**.32; **215**.11; **259**.5
job adverts
    and age discrimination **239**.12
    false **263**.29
job applications
    graduates **263**.24-5; **264**.35, 37
    response of Sherlock Holmes museum **263**.30
jobs
    and population growth **220**.6
    see also employment; labour market
Jobseeker's Allowance Claimant Commitment **263**.9
Joffe, Lord Joel, assisted dying campaign **217**.2
Johns, Owen and Eunice **215**.25, 26; **225**.34
jokes and banter as indirect racism **236**.28
journalists
    female **210**.7
    regulation **210**.27-8
journals and the grieving process **267**.13

Judaism and war and peace **259**.4
judicial system
    ethnic minorities in legal profession **236**.11-12
    treatment of ethnic minorities **236**.9-10
    see also criminal justice system
junk food
    advertising **241**.20, 21; **271**.27-30
    and supermarkets, survey **271**.37
Just War **259**.3, 4, 5
justice system
    and human rights abuses against children **268**.15
    see also criminal justice system
juvenile offenders and the death penalty **229**.38

K

Kami-Umtan-To (Chinese medicine) and dementia **269**.22
keeping fit *see* fitness
Kenya
    mobile learning support for young mothers **257**.38-9
    poaching **260**.10-11
    population growth **220**.2
Kervorkian, Dr Jack (Dr Death) **217**.2
ketamine **228**.5
    'legal high' alternative **228**.6
    possession, sentencing guidelines **228**.29-30
keyhole surgery **251**.2
kidneys, effects of alcohol **254**.3, 6
knife crime **223**.5, 25, 34
    discussion in schools **223**.16-17
    mandatory custodial sentences **223**.21, 25
    preventing **223**.34
    Scotland **223**.6-7
Knut the polar bear **233**.25
Kony 2012 campaign **266**.29, 38
Kosher meat **233**.16
Korsakoff's syndrome **201**.10
Kyoto Protocol **216**.34, 37
    and transport emissions **200**.15

L

labelling
    of disabled people **255**.9
    GM food **208**.8
    nanomaterials **208**.16
    tobacco products **261**.27
    see also food labelling
Labour Force Survey **263**.2
labour market
    decline of mid-range jobs **219**.39
    fairness in jobs market **219**.18-19, 20
    and graduates **264**.32-4
    and youth employment **263**.19-20
labour migration *see* migrant workers
lacto-vegetarians **214**.2
lads' magazines and pornography **238**.18
Lake of Stars **240**.35

Laming Review **248**.1
land grabs and human rights **229**.10
landfill **242**.5
    policy targets **242**.3
    waste of valuable materials **242**.7
landlords, regulation **253**.11, 12-13
landmines **259**.9, 39
lap dancing clubs **246**.23
large families and benefits **263**.8
Latin America, internally displaced persons **259**.18
Latvia, smoking ban **261**.31
law
    and abortion **231**.1-2, 3, 32
      and disability **231**.20
    and alcohol, drinking age **254**.21
    animal cloning **211**.11
    animal welfare **233**.1-2, 5-6
    anti-terrorism **212**.19, 20
    and assisted suicide **217**.24-38
      arguments against **217**.27
      arguments for **217**.29
      in other countries **217**.2
      in UK **217**.24-6
    and cannabis **256**.1-2, 27-39
    and child protection **248**.1, 34, 35-6
    cigarette sales **261**.3
    and cyberbullying **232**.34-5, 37
    and domestic violence **224**.28-9
    drinking age **254**.21
    and drug driving **228**.26
    and drugs **228**.13, 21-39
      sentencing guidelines **228**.28-31
      see also classification of drugs
    and environmental justice **218**.3, 4
    and euthanasia **217**.24-39
    and film classification **196**.14
    food from cloned animals **211**.12
    and forced marriages **224**.14-15
    and herbal medicines **269**.13-14, 15
    and HIV transmission **243**.11
    and homelessness **262**.3, 9
    human cloning **211**.25
    human rights *see* Human Rights Act
    and LGBT people **224**.13; **225**.6-7, 28-39
    libel law reform **210**.37
    and marriage **244**.1-3, 5, 8-9
    and privacy **245**.1-10
    and prostitution **246**.17-19, 21-3
    and religious belief **215**.26-7; **225**.34, 35
    and sexual consent **237**.12-14
    and smoking, children **252**.38-9
    and squatting **262**.13
    and surrogacy **247**.19
    and synthetic cannabinoids **256**.4
    and work-related stress **206**.25, 28-9
    see also legislation
laws of war **259**.1, 7-8
laxative use in eating disorders **249**.2
'learn as you earn' courses **264**.6
learning
    effects of cannabis **256**.11
    and happiness **265**.39
    learning styles **209**.1-3

learning disabilities **255**.2-3
    definitions **255**.2, 41
    and forced marriage **244**.12
    housing for people with learning disabilities **255**.13-14
    and police interviews **255**.30
    see also disabled people
leather and vegetarianism **214**.13
leave, Army **213**.2
Leeds, Greenhouse project **253**.37
Legal Aid, Sentencing and Punishment of Offenders Act **223**.25
    and squatting **262**.13
legal high drugs **228**.1, 36-8
    classification **228**.21
    deaths **252**.32
    and legislation **228**.26-7
    methoxetamine **228**.6
legal profession and ethnic minorities **236**.11-12
legal rights
    and gender equality **221**.2, 3, 35, 36
    at work **263**.4-5
    see also rights
legalising brothels **246**.26
legalising drugs
    arguments for **228**.34
    cannabis **256**.30-38
legalising prostitution, effects on trafficking **246**.29
legislation
    Civil Partnership Act **244**.18
    Communications Data Bill **245**.5-8
    Data Protection Act **245**.11
    Equal Pay Act **221**.35-6
    Equality Act **221**.3, 36; **225**.6
    Gender Recognition Act **225**.6, 20, 27
    Marriage (Same Sex Couples) Bill **244**.19-20
    Race Relations Act **236**.1-3, 16, 21
leisure activities
    and mental health **252**.25-6
    merging with work **263**.38-9
    Middle Britain **219**.2
    and young people's drinking habits **254**.30-31
Lennox (dog) **233**.12-13
lesbian, gay, bisexual and transgender *see* LGBT people
lesbians
    and ageing **239**.10-11
    and domestic violence **224**.5, 12-13
    human rights **229**.31-2
    young people, mental health problems **201**.3
    see also homosexuality; same-sex relationships
Let Girls Be Girls campaign **238**.8-9
lethal autonomous robots **259**.12
Letting Children be Children (Bailey Review) **238**.2, 5-7, 8, 33, 34
LGBT people **225**.1-39
    attitudes to **225**.11-13
    in children's books **257**.16
    equality policies, EU **225**.12-13
    and forced marriage **244**.12
    and the law **225**.28-39
    opinions on same sex marriage **244**.28
    and schools **225**.5-8
    and social exclusion **225**.9

and sports **270**.1-2, 16-19

transgender issues **225**.19-27

see also gay men; lesbians; same-sex relationships; sexual orientation

libel

libel actions, celebrities **210**.38

libel laws reform **210**.37

liberalization of trade   *see* free trade

Libya, conflict effects on children **259**.26, 39

licence periods (prison sentences) **223**.19-20, 21

LIFE, arguments against HPV vaccination **237**.29-31

life expectancy **239**.1, 3

and genes **239**.2

and homelessness **262**.20-21, 32

and obesity **241**.15

and population growth prediction **220**.9

and poverty **219**.13

life sentences **223**.20, 21

lifestyle

and health **219**.12

and healthcare rationing **261**.22-3

middle classes **219**.1-2, 9-10

and obesity **271**.9

and stress **206**.18, 32-4

students **209**.30-33

lifetime social tenancies **253**.15

light exposure at night and depression **265**.13

light rail **200**.30, 33-4

light therapy

and dementia treatment **269**.21

for Seasonal Affective Disorder **265**.11

lion hunting **260**.29, 30-31

literacy, women, worldwide **221**.37

litter **242**.13, 17

'live for today' attitude **250**.4

liver, effects of alcohol **254**.3, 5

Liverpool Care Pathway **251**.15

living together *see* cohabitation

living wage for garment industry workers **229**.13

living wills *see* advance directives (living wills)

Loaded magazine **238**.18

loans **235**.11-12

to entrepreneurs in developing countries **235**.33

payday loans **250**.5, 6

student **250**.22-5

see also credit; debt

local authorities

approved premises for marriages **244**.2

and ending violence against women and girls **224**.29

home building target reduction **253**.27

open data policy, Manchester **245**.12

priority need housing **262**.3, 9

responsibilities for under 16s **224**.37

selling properties to fund new home building **253**.29-30

social housing **253**.13-15

Local Authority Social Services Act 1970 **248**.35

local communities

action on responsible drinking **254**.20

effects of tourism **222**.21-3, 29-30, 33-4

and youth drinking cultures **254**.29-31

Local Safeguarding Children's Boards **224**.37

logbook loans **235**.12

loggerhead turtles **260**.1

loitering and soliciting **246**.21

London

bombings **212**.4, 5

congestion charge **200**.17-18

as graduate employment destination **263**.25

Olympics

and sex trafficking **229**.20

and tourism **222**.12-13

public transport **200**.30

rough sleepers **262**.32, 36

lone parents *see* single parent families

loneliness

and money worries **250**.33

older people **239**.8, 35, 36-7

living with HIV/AIDS **243**.19-20

and stress **206**.18

long-term medical conditions **252**.2, 3, 7-8

and financial insecurity **263**.16

see also asthma; cancer; diabetes

long-term workless households **263**.6, 13-14

Los Angeles, porn film regulations **246**.5

losing weight *see* weight loss

lotteries **203**.4

see also National Lottery

love and marriage **244**.4

Lovelock, James **220**.12

low income countries **235**.28-30

low income households **235**.5-8

see also child poverty

low income threshold **235**.5

low pay **235**.6

low volume high-intensity training **241**.27-8

loyalty cards and personal data **245**.18-19

lung cancer

and cannabis use **256**.8, 21

people unaware of symptoms **261**.16

lung damage

and alcohol **254**.5

and smoking **261**.1, 8

Luxembourg

assisted dying legislation **217**.2

smoking ban **261**.31

Lynx deodorant, advertisements **234**.22

M

M4 bus lane **200**.36

macrobiotic diets **269**.4

magazines

airbrushing in *Healthy* magazine **234**.27-8

display of sexualized images **238**.5

diversity award **234**.38

and eating disorders **249**.27, 28

UK magazine sector **210**.2-3

Vogue and body image **234**.5-6

see also lads' magazines

magnetic resonance imaging (MRI) as alternative to animal research **233**.32

maintenance grants and loans, students **250**.23-4

major (clinical) depression **265**.1

Malawi, withdrawal of aid due to anti-gay laws **225**.14

Maldives
impact of sea level rise **220**.38
impact of tourism **222**.23
male-bonding ceremonies **244**.5
malnutrition **271**.5
see also hunger
Malthus, Thomas **220**.3, 11, 14
management
gender gap **221**.19-20
glass ceiling **221**.21-2
Manchester city council, open data policy **245**.12
Mandate Now coalition **248**.38
Mandate to the NHS Commissioners Board **251**.27-8
mandatory life sentences **223**.21
mandatory reporting of child abuse **248**.37, 38
manic depression *see* bipolar affective disorder
manipulative therapies *see* chiropractice;
osteopathy
Many Strong Voices (MSV) project **216**.16
Maplecroft Human Rights Risk Atlas **229**.9
mapping genes **208**.13
margin of appreciation, European Court of Human
Rights **229**.6
marijuana *see* cannabis
Marine and Coastal Access Act **218**.22
marine environments
impacts of tourism **222**.25
and plastic waste **242**.21, 26-7
protection **218**.22-3
threats to **218**.24-5
marketing
and gender stereotyping **238**.34
junk food to children **271**.27-30
parental concerns **238**.35
and sexualisation of children **238**.6-7, 35
tobacco products, and children **261**.33, 39
see also advertising
marriage **244**.1-16
benefits **244**.10
ceremonies **244**.1-2
child marriage **244**.15; **248**.24-5; **268**.28-30
and civil partnerships **225**.35
common law marriage **244**.8-9
ending *see* divorce
forced marriages **224**.3, 14-15, 36-7; **244**.3,
12-14
and Islam **215**.12
history of **244**.4-5, 8-9
and Islam **215**.12
and law **244**.1-3, 5, 8-9
same-sex couples **225**.33; **244**.16-29
and stepfamilies *see* stepfamilies
and transsexuals **225**.27
worldwide trends **257**.3, 4-5
Marriage Act 1753 **244**.9
Marriage (Same Sex Couples) Bill **244**.19-20
masking agents (sports) **270**.32
massage and dementia treatment **269**.22
Massively Multiplayer Online Role-Playing Games
(MMORPG) **266**.1
match fixing, football **270**.33
maternal (metaphase) spindle transfer **247**.29, 31
maturity as a factor in sentencing young people **223**.33-4

Mayhew Animal Home **233**.1
MDMA *see* ecstasy
mealtimes and recovering anorexics **249**.37
Measure B (Safer Sex in the Adult Film Industry Act) **246**.5
meat consumption
meat substitutes **214**.9, 11
need to reduce **214**.15-16, 22-3, 24, 27
nutrients **214**.34-5
red meat and health **214**.34-5
Meat Free Mondays campaign **214**.27
meat production
arguments for and against **214**.18-21
from cloned cows **211**.12, 15-17
and the environment **214**.16, 17, 18-19, 20-21
intensively farming **233**.3, 7-8
laboratory-grown meat **211**.20-21
large-scale pig farms **233**.11
sustainable **214**.14, 20-21, 23
media **210**.1-39
and body image **234**.5, 7, 8, 10, 11, 18
and celebrities as role models **238**.13
climate change reporting **216**.22-4
disabled people portrayal **255**.10-11
and eating disorders **249**.15, 25-31
employment of ethnic minorities **236**.11
and gambling **203**.26
guidelines for reporting suicide and self-harm **258**.1
and Islamophobia **215**.33; **236**.23-4
and mental ill health **201**.23; **265**.7
misleading reporting of cannabis studies **256**.
25-6
multi-tasking **210**.11
new technologies **210**.13-26
and the permissive society **196**.25-6
and privacy **210**.33-9
public opinion on media freedom **229**.12
regulation **210**.27-9, 34
and religion **215**.13
representation of young people **239**.6
and Scottish Gypsy Travellers **236**.22
and sexualisation of children **238**.3, 13, 32-3
trends **210**.1-12
violence *see* violence, media
WikiLeaks **210**.20-26
and women's sport **270**.20-22
see also broadcasters; films; Internet; magazines;
newspapers; press; radio; telecommunications;
television
medical abortion **231**.7
medical ethics argument against euthanasia **217**.4
medical insurance **251**.5-6
and use of NHS **251**.7
medical profession
and assisted suicide **217**.22, 24-5
effects of legalizing assisted dying **217**.4, 8, 11, 31
see also doctors
medical research, use of animals **233**.28-39
medical students and debt **264**.20
medical treatment
cannabis use **256**.19, 20, 29
injured service personnel **213**.2, 8-9, 10-11
patient's right to refuse **217**.13, 25
self-harm injuries **258**.5, 15

withdrawing **217**.14

see also complementary and alternative medicine; palliative care

medically-assisted dying *see* physician-assisted suicide

medicines

from GM plants **208**.21-2

from GM animals **208**.13

and obesity **241**.16

for stress and anxiety **206**.3, 13

see also antidepressant drugs; drug treatments; drugs; herbal medicines

Medicines and Healthcare Products Regulatory Agency and homeopathy **269**.12

mega-farms **233**.9-11

megafauna **260**.34

Megan's Law **248**.35

Members of Parliament *see* MPs

memories of the deceased *see* remembrance of the deceased

memory boxes **267**.13

men

and abortion **231**.9

body image concerns **234**.13, 16-17

cannabis use **256**.15

career aspirations **221**.21

and compulsive shopping **207**.6

as domestic abuse victims **224**.5, 9-10, 11

and eating disorders **249**.3, 4-5, 15, 18-19

fertility

and age **247**.6

fertility drugs **247**.9

problems **247**.2

and household tasks **221**.6; **263**.15

and HPV vaccine **237**.27

Internet usage **230**.3-4

and IVF procedure **247**.10

media usage **210**.12

men deserts **257**.12

paternity leave **221**.4-5

and prostitution **246**.24-5

and sexually transmitted infections **237**.19, 22

suicide rate **258**.33

symptoms of stress **206**.7-8

talking about problems **265**.28

as victims of trafficking **246**.39

see also boys and young men; fathers; gay men

Mendel, Gregor **211**.2

Mental Capacity Act and right to refuse medical treatment **217**.13

mental function, effects of cannabis **256**.22-4

mental health **252**.13-26

and abortion **231**.14-15

and alcohol **254**.1, 3, 5, 6

benefits of exercise **241**.4, 33-4

and body image **234**.10, 11, 19

and cannabis **228**.8; **256**.11-12, 20, 32

schizophrenia **256**.11-12, 34, 35-6

children, and aggression **224**.23

and homeless people **262**.2, 14, 19

improving **201**.33-4, 35-6; **265**.38-9

and social media **266**.27

statistics, young people **252**.2

and stress **206**.36-7

strategies **201**.5, 35

and urban green spaces **265**.35

young people **252**.2, 13-26

see also dementia; depression

Mental Health Act **201**.38-9

mental health services **201**.5

insufficiencies **201**.37

and young people **201**.10-11, 36

mental illness **201**.1-39

and Armed Forces personnel **213**.3-4, 5, 6

attitudes to **201**.22-3, 31

and cannabis **228**.8

causes **201**.32-3

children **201**.2-4

costs **201**.1, 23

and domestic violence **224**.7

ex-service personnel **213**.33-4

and gambling **203**.37

and homosexuality **201**.3

and malnutrition **271**.5

prevalence **201**.5, 6

and social welfare problems **201**.29

stigma **201**.22-3, 31

self-stigma **201**.28

young carers **201**.8

and suicide **258**.21

young people **201**.2-4, 7, 29-30

see also bipolar affective disorder; dementia; depression; post-traumatic stress disorder; schizophrenia

mental symptoms

of anxiety **206**.10

of stress **206**.1-2, 9, 19

mentoring

and applications to university **264**.5

of girls **221**.32

of young people by ex-service personnel **213**.32

mephedrone (meow meow) **228**.23, 36, 37

classification **228**.21-2, 23, 32

deaths **252**.32

mercy killing *see* non-voluntary euthanasia

Messi, Lionel **270**.10-11

metabolically healthy obese people **241**.17

metal waste exports, EU **242**.18

metaphase (maternal) spindle transfer **247**.29, 31

methamphetamine (crystal meth) **228**.23

methane

as car fuel **204**.39

emissions from biodegradable products **218**.37

Methodist Church and abortion **231**.19

methoxetamine (MXE/Mexxy) **228**.6

metro systems **200**.34

Metropolitan Police and racism **236**.26

mica mines and child labour **268**.7-9

micro-blogging **266**.1

microdosing as alternative to animal research **233**.32

microfinance **235**.34-5

microgeneration of energy **204**.35-6

solar water heating **204**.21-2

water power **204**.19

Mid-Staffordshire NHS Foundation Trust public inquiry **251**.3, 4, 14-15, 16

middle-classes **219**.1-2, 9-10

Middle East
  criminalization of homosexuality **225**.39
  instability and prediction of future conflicts
    259.37
  internally displaced persons **259**.18
  press freedom **196**.2
  as tourist destination **222**.8
  see also individual countries
middle-income countries **235**.28-30
Middleton, Kate **232**.5-6
migraine, acupuncture treatment **269**.2
migrant children, UK **268**.18. 36-7
migrant families and child abuse **248**.22-3
migrant workers **220**.32-3
  agricultural work **263**.10-11
  East European, racism towards **236**.32
  integration **236**.17
  returning due to unemployment **220**.34
  women **220**.35
migration **220**.8-9, 20-39
  and climate change **220**.38, 39
  elimination of barriers, economic benefits **226**.39
  forced **220**.36-7; **259**.18-23
  and population growth **220**.9
  reasons for **220**.20, 36-7
  statistics **220**.21
  to UK **220**.20-21, 24-5
  of workforce (brain drain) **220**.32-3
  see also asylum seekers; immigration
mild cognitive impairment **239**.29
mild depression **265**.1
  treatment options **265**.22
military forces, USA, and sexual orientation **225**.
  38-9
military intervention
  Afghanistan **259**.32
  justification **259**.29, 35-6
Military to Mentors programme **213**.32
milk from cloned cows **211**.12, 13-14
Millennium Development Goals **226**.3; 1-2, 25-7
  2011 report **218**.39
  and disability **255**.39
  education **229**.27-8
  employment **235**.26
  hunger **235**.26-7
  poverty reduction **235**.25-6
  water and sanitation **218**.31, 36-7
Mind **241**.12
MindFull, online counselling support **258**.16
mindfulness-based cognitive therapy (MBCT)
  265.26
Mines Awareness Group (MAG) **259**.39
mini pill (contraception) **237**.6
minimum income standard **235**.3, 5
minimum unit pricing of alcohol **254**.14, 19, 37-8
minimum wage **263**.5-6
Ministers, government **240**.26
minority ethnic groups *see* ethnic minorities
minority rights **229**.24-39
Miras (mortgage interest tax relief) **253**.17
miscarriage and IVF **247**.7
missing children **248**.28
Misuse of Drugs Act 1971 **228**.21, 22, 24

  sentencing guidelines **228**.28-31
mitochondrial diseases prevented by three-parent
  IVF **247**.29-34
MMORPG (Massively Multiplayer Online Role-
  Playing Games) **266**.1
MMR vaccine and autism **255**.7
mobile phones
  and blogging **210**.16
  bullying by **232**.17, 25, 27, 29
  and education of young Kenyan mothers **257**.
    38-9
  and homeless people **262**.34-5
  and Internet access **230**.1
  and pornography access by children and young
people **238**.4, 19; **246**.11
  and relationship abuse **224**.20
  sexting **238**.23-4
  and social networking **210**.14
  usage trends **210**.11
    and gender **210**.12
    international comparison **210**.13-14
mockery as indirect racism **236**.28
modeling
  agencies targeting eating disorder sufferers **249**.26
  model dies of anorexia **234**.36
  and sexualisation of children **238**.27-8
  teenagers **234**.35; **238**.38
Modern Classic families **257**.8
monarchy, UK **240**.22-3
  arguments against **240**.24-5
money
  money management *see* financial skills
  students *see* students and money matters
  see also banks; credit; debt; finance; incomes;
wages
money worries
  children **250**.20
  and depression **265**.2
  and health **250**.29, 33
  new parents **257**.28
  and stress **206**.18, 21, 39
Mongolia, education programme **229**.28
Monitor (NHS regulator) **251**.25-6, 31
monoamine oxidase inhibitors (MAOIs) **265**.20
moral character development through sport **270**.5-6
moral rights of embryos **211**.31, 34
morality and business **227**.22-3
morning after pill *see* emergency contraception
mortality
  Armed Forces mortality rate **213**.9
  benefits of reflection on mortality **267**.26
  homeless people **262**.20, 32
  and population trends **220**.9
  see also deaths; life expectancy
mortgage guarantee scheme (Help to Buy) **253**.8, 25
mortgage interest tax relief (Miras) **253**.17
mosques as targets of hate crime **215**.29
motherhood role and the abortion debate **231**.18-19
mothers
  in the Army **213**.13-14
  education via mobiles for young Kenyan mothers
    257.38-9
  HIV transmission to children **243**.1-2, 25

as migrant workers **220**.35
and pay gap **221**.24
putting images of young children on social
networking sites **266**.23
teenage mothers **257**.32-3, 35-9
see also working mothers
motoring *see* cars; driving
motorways
M4 bus lane **200**.36
motorway phobia **200**.4
motorway travel frequency **200**.5
mourning *see* grief
mourning clothes **267**.12
movies *see* films
MPs
ethnic minority **236**.11
female **221**.13, 15, 20
MRI (magnetic resonance imaging) as alternative to
animal research **233**.32
MSN, children's use of **245**.25
Muamba, Fabrice, subject of Twitter racism **236**.31
Multilateral Investment Guarantee Agency (MIGA) **226**.10
multinational corporations (MNCs) **226**.1, 27
and tax **227**.32-3
multiple births and fertility treatment **247**.4
multiple sclerosis (MS)
cannabis treatment **256**.19
stem cell treatment **211**.38-9
muscle dysmorphic disorder (bigorexia) **249**.7
musculoskeletal health and physical activity **241**.4-5
music therapy and dementia treatment **269**.22
music videos
age ratings **238**.5
sexual content **238**.20-22
Muslims
anti-Muslim hate crime **215**.28-30; **236**.14, 24
British **215**.9-12; **240**.17-18
discrimination against **215**.30, 31-2
female basketball player and hijab ban **270**.24-5
media portrayal **236**.23-4
Muslim extremists, protests against British
soldiers **196**.9-10
public attitudes to **212**.4, 30-31; **215**.33
ritual slaughter **233**.16
as stop and search targets **212**.28-9
veiling of Muslim women **215**.34-8
see also Islam; Islamophobia
My Money Week education project **250**.17
Myanmar
child labour **268**.10
forced labour **229**.15
MySpace, reporting inappropriate content **232**.35

N

NAMA (non-agricultural market access) **226**.15-16
name-calling, dealing with **232**.19-20
nanotechnology **208**.15-16
narcissism and social media **266**.9-10
National Assembly for Wales **240**.27
National Canine Defence League (NCDL) **233**.1
National Careers Service (NCS) **264**.4

National Child Measurement Programme **241**.24
National Citizen Service programme **240**.33-4
National Commissioning Board (NHS) **251**.25
National Crime Agency **223**.22
National Curriculum and enterprise education **263**.
28-9
National DNA Database **245**.14-15
National Health Service *see* NHS
national identity
British *see* British identity
and globalization **226**.12
National Institute for Clinical Excellence (NICE) *see*
NICE
National Insurance **250**.15
National Lottery
children participating **203**.12-13
online participation **203**.4
National Minimum Wage **263**.5-6
national origins
of British Olympic athletes **240**.10-11
of UK population **240**.15-16
National Student Survey (NSS) **264**.27
natural gas, industry trends **204**.1
natural medicine *see* complementary and alternative
medicine; herbal medicine
natural remedies **269**.26-7
natural resources consumption **218**.7-8, 13-14
impact of global development **226**.3-4
impact of tourism **222**.29
water **218**.33
nausea, acupuncture treatment **269**.2
Nazareth, Colombia, ban on tourists **222**.32
neck pain, acupuncture treatment **269**.2
needle sharing and HIV transmission **243**.1
NEETs (young people not in employment, education
or training) **252**.21
negative body image *see* body image, negative
neglect **248**.3, 14-20
law reform **248**.35
neonatal death **267**.22
Netherlands, The
assisted dying legislation **217**.2, 9, 11
cannabis legalisation **256**.30-31
elderly people's fears of euthanasia **217**.33
health care **251**.9
LGBT equality policy **225**.13
sex education **237**.33-4
neurobiology and sexual orientation **225**.15-16
New Horizons programme (NHS) **251**.3
New Strategic Direction for Alcohol and Drugs
(N.Ireland) **228**.24
New York
law on marijuana possession **256**.21
raising tobacco purchase age **261**.30
New Zealand, cannabis laws **256**.29
NewBuy **253**.8
news media
and social media **266**.28-9
and women **210**.6-8
female presenters and reporters **210**.7
women as news subjects **210**.6, 7-8
News of the World, phone-hacking **210**.35-6
newspapers **210**.1-2
display of sexualized images **238**.5

ownership **210**.2
paid-for websites **210**.19
regulations **210**.27-8
NGOs (non-governmental organisations) **226**.1, 4
NHS (National Health Service) **219**.12; **251**.1-10
age discrimination ban **239**.11
and complementary and alternative medicine
269.19
constitution **251**.3, 4, 27-8
costs of overweight and obesity **241**.3
depression treatment statistics **265**.25
funding **251**.1, 36
funding crisis **251**.34-5, 38
public opinions **251**.20-21
history **251**.2-4
and homeopathy **269**.34-5, 36
international comparisons **251**.8, 9
and IVF treatment **247**.10, 22-5
open data policy **245**.12-13
post traumatic stress disorder treatment **213**.3-4
public opinions **251**.19-22
quality of care **251**.8, 11-13, 33
reform **251**.25-39
size **251**.1
staff survey **251**.18
Stop Smoking service **261**.10, 24
structure **251**.1, 4, 25-6, 29, 30-32
NHS and Community Care Act **251**.3
NHS Direct **251**.3
NHS England **251**.4, 30
NICE (National Institute for Clinical Excellence)
251.26
guidelines on complementary and alternative
medicine **269**.19
guidelines on IVF **247**.10, 22-5, 27
nicotine **261**.3, 4, 5
Nigeria, kidnapped schoolgirls social media
campaign **266**.38
night shelters see hostels for homeless people
nights out
safety **254**.35-6
young people's drinking habits **254**.30
niqab, arguments for and against wearing **215**.37-8
no make-up selfies **266**.35, 36
No Second Night Out **262**.37, 38
noise
from traffic **200**.14-15, 22
from wind turbines **204**.12
non-agricultural market access (NAMA) **226**.15-16
non-governmental organisations (NGOs) **226**.1, 4
non-reproductive cloning see therapeutic cloning
non-violence and religions **259**.3-4
non-voluntary euthanasia **217**.5
Kay Inglis **217**.27, 29
Nordic countries, criminality of prostitution **246**.20
North Korea
death penalty **229**.37
nuclear weapons **259**.14-15
North London Cares **239**.38
northern bald ibis **260**.1-2
Northern Ireland
abortion law **231**.3, 25
drug strategy **228**.24

and national identity **240**.12
Northern Ireland Assembly **240**.27
Republican terrorist groups **212**.14
young people's sexual lifestyles **237**.15-17
Norway, exporting waste to Sweden **242**.37
novel psychoactive substances see legal high drugs
novels about teenage suicide **258**.30
NSPCC **252**.15
How Safe are our Children? report **248**.7
report on children missing from care homes **248**.2
nuclear families **257**.1-2
Nuclear Non-Proliferation Treaty **259**.10
nuclear power **204**.26
political support for **216**.25
nuclear weapons **259**.14-15
nurses giving sex education lessons **237**.34
nutrition
and GM crops **208**.35-6
malnutrition **271**.5
see also hunger
and meat **214**.34-5
nutrition labelling **271**.26, 33
Quorn products **214**.9
and veganism **214**.3
and vegetarianism **214**.28-39
see also diet; healthy eating
nutritional supplements and malnutrition **271**.5

O2, criticism of Communications Data Bill **245**.6
O'Dell, Michael (video gamer) **270**.35-6
Obama, Barack
and closure of Guantánamo Bay **212**.33, 34-5
defending use of drones **259**.12
obesity and overweight **241**.2-3, 14-24; **271**.6-7, 8-9
avoidance see weight management
causes **241**.15-16
in children see childhood obesity
government strategies **271**.6-7, 9
and health **241**.15, 17; **271**.9, 20
and life expectancy **241**.15
restricting healthcare treatment of obese people **261**.
22-3
statistics **241**.2-3, 15
treatment costs **241**.3, 18-19
and young people **252**.2
see also body weight; weight management
Obscene Publications Acts **196**.14, 22; **246**.7
obscenity **196**.22-3
oceans, threats to **218**.24-5
occupational pensions **250**.12
occupational segregation **221**.19, 27-9
Ofcom **196**.18-20
Broadcasting Code **210**.27
and offensive language on television **196**.21, 24
Offences against the Person Act 1861 **231**.1
Offender Discrimination Act **223**.27
offenders
recovery programmes **223**.23-4
and restorative justice **223**.28-9

see also ex-offenders
offensive language on television **196**.21, 24
offensive material
    broadcasters' rights **196**.24
    cartoons in airport prayer room **196**.11-12
offsetting carbon *see* carbon offsetting
offshore wind power **204**.14-18
Ofsted and sexuality equality legislation **225**.7
OHSS (ovarian hyper-stimulation syndrome) **247**.7
oil
    arguments against production **204**.9-10
    industry trends **204**.1
older people
    abuse of **224**.4; **239**.4, 34
    as an asset **239**.16
    care *see* care services for older people
    causes of death **267**.20
    communications trends **210**.11-12
    and dementia *see* dementia
    disabled, financial concerns **255**.22-3
    and HIV /AIDS **243**.18-19
    and health **239**.4, 8, 10, 24-39
    health benefits of dance **241**.33-4
    hospital care **251**.11-13
    in employment *see* older workers
    Internet usage **230**.5, 19-21
    lesbian, gay and bisexual people **239**.10
    physical activity recommendations **241**.6
    and poverty **235**.6, 8; **239**.8, 17, 18
    shared ownership housing scheme **253**.8
    retirement *see* retirement
    and social media **266**.16
    and sport **270**.1
    and suicide **258**.24
    wellbeing **239**.8-9, 13
    see also age discrimination; ageing population;
grandparents
older women and IVF **247**.10, 22-6
older workers **239**.16, 18; **263**.31-2
    and financial insecurity **263**.16
Olympic Games
    foreign-born athletes in Team GB **240**.10-11
    London, opening ceremony, use of animals **233**.13
    Olympic athletes visiting schools and
communities **270**.7
    and pride in Britain **240**.9
    and sex trafficking **229**.20
    sporting legacy **241**.9, 10
    and tourist industry **222**.12-13
    see also Paralympic Games
omega 3 fatty acids **214**.29, 33
one-child rule, China **220**.4, 18
one-parent families *see* lone parents
online bullying *see* cyberbullying
online divorce services **244**.34, 35
online gambling **203**.28-9
    participation rates **203**.4
    women **203**.35-6
    young people **203**.16-18
online games and junk food marketing **271**.28,
    29-30
online grooming **230**.23-4
online multiplayer gaming **266**.1
online personal data

children's **245**.16
    consumer awareness **245**.17-19
    dealing with accounts after a death **267**.37-8
    protection **245**.20; **266**.7, 18
    and risk of fraud **245**.21-2
online persona **266**.6
online pornography *see* Internet pornography
online racism **236**.31
online reputation **230**.31-2; **266**.7, 18
online retail *see* Internet shopping
online safety *see* safety and the Internet
online socialising *see* social networking
online trade in protected wildlife and ivory **260**.17-18,
20
online travel booking **222**.3
open data policy **245**.12-13
oral sex and safety **237**.3
orang-utans **260**.26
Orbach, Susie **234**.5, 7-8
Oregon State, assisted dying legislation **217**.2, 11
Oreo, complaints about marketing to children
271.30
organ donation
    from euthanasia victims **217**.32
    opt-out scheme in Wales **267**.39
    Organ Donation Register **251**.3
organ harvesting and human trafficking **229**.18
organ transplants *see* therapeutic cloning
organic food **214**.23, 29
    consumer attitudes **207**.30
organic waste
    energy generation **204**.6
    gas production **204**.24
orthorexia nervosa **249**.8
osteoarthritis **239**.26; **241**.4-5
osteopathy **269**.3, 8
osteoporosis **239**.26; **241**.4-5
out-of-school children **268**.22-3
outsourcing of Internet control **196**.33-4
ovarian hyper-stimulation syndrome (OHSS) **247**.7
overall poverty **235**.1
overdoses *see* drug overdoses
overnutrition **271**.5
overseas adoption **247**.15, 17
overseas surrogacy arrangements **247**.19
overseas travel, attitudes to **222**.2
    see also tourism
overweight people   *see* obesity and overweight
overwork **263**.32, 36, 37-8
ovo-vegetarians **214**.2
ovulation problems **247**.1
    and fertility drugs **247**.8-9
ownership, newspapers **210**.2
Oxford child trafficking case **246**.37

P

paan (chewing tobacco) **261**.10
Pacific Ocean, marine debris **242**.21
pacifism **259**.3-4, 5
    and Christianity **259**.4
packaging, cigarettes **261**.27, 35

pain and depression **239**.32
pain relief
   and the placebo effect **269**.37
   see also palliative care
Pakistan
   children in prison **268**.14
   population growth **220**.2
Palermo Protocol (prevention of trafficking) **229**.17
palliative care **217**.10, 15-17, 18, 38; **267**.18-19, 25
   and assisted dying **217**.11, 17
   availability **217**.15-16
   and complementary therapies **269**.23
   effectiveness **217**.16
   limitations **217**.10, 11, 16
   Scotland **217**.18
palliative sedation **217**.3, 14, 25
palm oil industry and destruction of tiger habitat
   260.12
pancreas, effects of alcohol **254**.5
panic attacks **206**.11, 16
Papadopoulos, Dr Linda (psychologist) **238**.10-12
paper layer of privacy **245**.2-3
Paralympic Games **255**.41
   impact on disabled people **255**.17; **270**.12-13, 14
   Paralympic athletes visiting schools and
communities **270**.7
   and public attitude to disabled people **255**.15-16;
      270.12-13
Parasport website **270**.14
parental leave **221**.4-5, 24
   for adoption **247**.16
parental orders and surrogacy **247**.19
parental separation **257**.11-12
   costs of family breakdown **257**.11
   effect on children **244**.36-7; **257**.12, 13
   and grandparents' rights **257**.18-20
   online help **244**.34
parenting orders **223**.32
parents
   and alcohol, allowing children to taste **254**.32
   attitudes to school learning styles **209**.1-3
   and children's aggression **224**.22-3
   and children's body image **234**.10
   and children's education attainment **219**.26, 27, 33
   and children's gambling **203**.13
   and children's Internet activity **238**.5, 25; **246**.15; **245**.
      26-7
   and children's obesity **241**.20, 23
   of disabled children, experiencing stigma **255**.25-8
   health advice source for young people **252**.4-5
   of lesbians and gays **225**.3-4
   with mental health problems, effects on children
      201.4, 8-9
   money worries **257**.28
   parenting tips **257**.24
   in prison, effects on children **201**.4
   putting pressure on schools **209**.4
   same-sex parents **257**.14-18
   satisfaction with schools **209**.21
   and sexualisation of children
      concerns about **238**.7, 10, 14, 20, 35
      encouraging **238**.36-7
   of sexually exploited children **248**.31

and social media **266**.21
   concerns about children's use **266**.19
   uploading images of young children **266**.23
stress due to long working hours **206**.22-3
and student finance **250**.24
support for children's education **209**.36
teaching financial skills **250**.21
teenage parents **257**.32-9
using pension to help children buy homes **253**.17
see also divorce; families; fathers; lone parents;
mothers; working parents
Paris Commitments and Principles on child soldiers
   268.24, 25-6
Parkinson's disease and animal research **233**.36, 38
parks, fitness equipment **241**.36-7
Parliament **240**.3, 25
   ethnic minority members **236**.11
   Scottish **240**.27
   women members **221**.13, 15, 20, 37
part-time jobs
   and the gender pay gap **221**.24, 28
   students **209**.32
parties, political *see* political parties
passive euthanasia **217**.5
passive smoking **261**.1, 14
   in cars carrying children **261**.28-9
   children **252**.38
passive victims of bullying **232**.8
pasteurization **211**.2
patents on GM seeds **208**.3-4
paternity leave **221**.4-5
pathological gambling *see* problem gambling
patients
   elderly patients' care **251**.11-13
   rights to choice **251**.3, 26
   rights to refuse treatment **217**.13, 25
patriotic hacking **196**.34-5
patriotism and the Union Jack **240**.4-5
pay gap
   ethnic **236**.18
   gender **221**.22-5, 27-8, 35-6, 37
payday loans **235**.11; **250**.5, 6
PAYE (Pay As You Earn) **250**.13
payment methods trends **250**.3
PCC *see* Press Complaints Commission
PCOS (polycystic ovary syndrome) **247**.1
peace negotiations, female participation **221**.37
Peace Pledge Union **259**.5
peacekeeping operations, UN **259**.37, 38
   and use of drones **259**.13
peer pressure and marijuana use **256**.5
peer support for eating disorders **249**.20
pelvic inflammatory disease **247**.2
penalties
   dealing cannabis **256**.27
   possession of cannabis **256**.2, 27-9
penguins, Galapagos **260**.38-9
pensions **239**.15, 19
   Army **213**.2
   concerns for disabled people **255**.22
   saving for **239**.14; **250**.36
   professional sports players **270**.8
   workplace pensions **250**.12

people smuggling **229**.18; **246**.30
Pepsi Cola, alcohol content **254**.34
periods, sex during **237**.3, 11
permissive behaviour, effect of the media **196**.25-6
persistent grief **267**.3-4, 6-7
Personal Independence Payment **263**.9
personal information **245**.11-27
    children's data held without parental consent
      245.16
    consumer concerns about online data **245**.17-19
    control of **230**.24, 30
    and Data Protection Act **245**.11
    protecting **245**.20
    and risk of fraud **245**.21-2
    see also online personal data
personal relationships *see* relationships
Personal, Social, Health and Economic (PSHE)
education
    covering sexualisation and gender stereotyping
      238.4, 11, 14
personality and social media **266**.6
pescetarian diet **214**.1
pest control and animal welfare **233**.4
pesticides and GM crops **208**.3, 21, 23
Petermann Glacier **216**.15
pets
    death of a pet **267**.8-10
    and passive smoking **261**.14
pharmaceutical industry and GM crops **208**.21-2
pharmaceutical waste and water pollution **218**.38-9
phased retirement **263**.33
philanthropy **227**.20-21
Philippines, horse fighting **233**.27
philosophical beliefs, Equality Act definition **215**.24
phishing **230**.30
phobias **206**.11
    in children **206**.13
    treatment **206**.12-13
phone-hacking **210**.35-6
photos, online accounts, after death **267**.38
Photoshopping *see* airbrushing
physical abuse
    of children **248**.3
    as domestic abuse **224**.1, 3
physical activity *see* exercise
physical education, government guidelines **271**.6
physician-assisted suicide (PAS)
    doctors' opposition to **217**.22
    prevalence **217**.24-5
    see also assisted suicide
phytomedicine **269**.21-2
pica **249**.8
Pick's disease **201**.10
pig farming, mega-farms **233**.10-11
Pilkington, Lesley **225**.17
pill, contraceptive **237**.6-7
pineapple as natural remedy **269**.27
PIPA (Protect IP Act) **230**.35-6, 37
piracy on the Internet **230**.35-6
placebo effect **269**.37
planning laws and inequality **218**.3, 4
planning permission reform **253**.27
plastic bags **242**.25-7
    used in road surfacing **242**.28

Plastic Brits (foreign-born athletes) **240**.10-11
plastic surgery *see* cosmetic surgery
plastic waste
    broken down by fungus **242**.27
    import ban by China **242**.21
    in Pacific Ocean **242**.21
    plastic bags **242**.25-7, 28
    recycling **242**.23, 24
Platform 51 **221**.28
pluripotent stem cells **211**.28, 35-7
    see also embryonic stem cells; iPS cells
poaching
    elephants **260**.9-11, 21, 23
    rhinos **260**.9-11
    tigers **260**.13-15; **269**.17
pocket money **250**.39
podcasting **266**.1
poker, online **203**.28-9
Poland, breaking EU law on herbal medicines
    269.14
police
    open data policy **245**.12
    and people with learning disabilities **255**.30
    and racism **236**.10, 26-7
    reporting a crime **223**.12
    reporting sexual assault **237**.13-14
    and Terrorism Act **212**.16
Policing and Crime Act and prostitution **246**.17,
    18-19
political correctness versus free speech **236**.35-7
political debates, inclusion of the BNP **196**.7, 8
political material, Ofcom regulation **196**.19
political parties, views on climate change **216**.25
politics
    and middle classes **219**.10
    recent British politics **240**.21
    women's participation **221**.2, 13, 15, 20, 37
    women's right to vote **221**.36
    young people's involvement **240**.39
      and the Internet **230**.9
    see also government; MPs; Parliament; voting
pollution
    effects of smoking and tobacco industry **261**.9
    see also emissions; water pollution
polycystic ovary syndrome (PCOS) **247**.1
polygamy **244**.3, 4
    and Islam **215**.12
polyols **271**.11
pools **203**.4
Poor Laws **219**.11
poorism (slum tourism) **222**.16, 33-4
POP (progestogen only pill) **237**.6-7
pop-culture tourism **222**.16
population *see* ageing population; population
growth
population growth **218**.26-30; **220**.1-15
    controlling **218**.26-7; **220**.4, 10, 16-17, 19
    developed countries **220**.1
    developing countries **220**.2, 4
    economic effects **220**.7
    effects **220**.4, 5-7
    and the environment **220**.4, 6-7, 14
    and food supply **218**.29-30; 3-4, 6
    growth rate **220**.1-2, 3, 13

projections **220**.2, 8-9
statistics **220**.4
and sustainability **218**.5
UK **220**.19
pornography **246**.1-16
   and children and young people **246**.10-11, 12
   education about **246**.12-13, 14
   effects **238**.16-26; **246**.1-2, 10-11, 12, 13
   and the Internet **238**.16, 19, 25, 26; **246**.3
      children viewing **196**.38; **238**.3-4, 14-15; **246**.10-11
      filters **246**.7-8, 15-16
      women viewing **230**.2-3
   and lads' magazines **238**.18
   and the law **246**.7-8, 9
   and mobile phones **238**.4, 19
   and prostitution **246**.24
   and women's choices **246**.3, 4-5
   see also child pornography
pornography industry **246**.11
   and women **246**.3, 4-5
   regulation, LA County **246**.5
Portugal
   decriminalisation of drugs possession **228**.34
   smoking ban **261**.31
positive action and age discrimination **239**.13
positive attitude and mental well-being **265**.2, 39
possession of drugs
   cannabis **228**.28-9; **256**.2, 27-9
   sentencing guidelines **228**.28-31
post-2015 development framework and child protection **248**.32-3
post-compulsory education
   see A-levels; higher education; universities
postgraduate destinations **264**.39
postnatal depression **265**.2, 12-13
post-traumatic stress disorder (PTSD) **201**.20-21
   service personnel **213**.3-4, 5
   therapies **213**.34
potatoes
   genetically modified **208**.11
   powering batteries **204**.39
poverty
   and child labour **268**.3
   and child marriage **268**.28
   children see child poverty
   definitions **235**.1, 2-3
   and disabled people **235**.5, 7
   and education **209**.13-14, 34-5; **235**.21-2
      pupil premium **209**.18
   food poverty **235**.17; **271**.3
   and free trade **226**.14, 29-30, 33
   fuel poverty see fuel poverty
   and girl's schooling **221**.39
   global **226**.17; **235**.23-39
   and mental health problems **201**.4
   and Millennium Development Goals **218**.39; **235**.1-2, 25-7
   and older people **235**.6, 8; **239**.8, 17, 18
   and population growth **220**.6
   reduction
      through migration **226**.39
      through trade **226**.28

rich-poor gap, UK **235**.12, 13
   and sport participation **241**.29
statistics **235**.5-8, 23, 24
and transport, developing countries **200**.13
in the UK **235**.1-22
and women **221**.34
see also child poverty; inequality
poverty cycle **235**.35
poverty tourism **222**.16, 33-4
power and control wheel **224**.7
power stations using biomass **204**.5, 7
Prader-Willi Syndrome **249**.8
Pratchett, Terry, assisted suicide documentary **217**.20
pre-implantation genetic testing **247**.8
pre-marital doubts and risk of divorce **244**.32-3
predators, declining populations **260**.6, 36-7
pregnancy **247**.1
   and alcohol **254**.8
   and complementary and alternative therapies **269**.38-9
   and domestic abuse **224**.4-5
      effects on unborn babies **224**.24, 37
   and eating disorders **249**.12
   and HIV diagnosis **243**.13
   and HIV transmission to baby **243**.1-2, 25
   myths about getting pregnant **237**.3, 4, 11, 35
   pregnancy options counselling **231**.36-7
   and sex education **237**.8
   and smoking **261**.1
   unplanned, statistics **237**.9-10
   see also abortion; teenage pregnancies
prejudice
   Islamaphobia see Islamophobia
   against working classes **219**.3-4, 5-6
   see also discrimination; homophobia; racial prejudice
premature babies
   premature births reduced following smoking ban **261**.32
   survival rate **231**.21, 22
prescriptions
   introduction of charges **251**.2
   for treating alcohol dependence **254**.10
press
   press freedom, global study **196**.1-2
   press self-regulation, public support for **196**.6
   Youth Parliament manifesto **240**.39
   see also media
Press Complaints Commission **196**.3, 4-5
   Editor's Code **210**.27-8
   reform proposals **210**.29
   statement on phone-hacking **210**.36
Pretty, Diane **217**.1-2, 24
Prevent strategy (anti-terrorism) **212**.17-18
Prevention of Cruelty to Children Acts **248**.35
Prevention of Terrorism Act 2005 **212**.19
price of alcohol, minimum unit pricing **254**.14, 19, 37-8
pricing
   Fairtrade prices **226**.36
   misleading practices **207**.15
Primark and sexualised clothes for children **238**.31
Primary Care Trusts (PCTs) **251**.3

abolition **251**.25
Prime Minister **240**.26
priority need housing **262**.3, 9
prison
    and children, Pakistan **268**.18-19
    and ex-service personnel **213**.4, 36, 37-9
    and the Human Rights Act **229**.5, 6
    and mental health, young people **201**.4
    prison sentences **223**.19-20, 21
        not a deterrent for knife crime **223**.34
    prisoners' right to vote **229**.35-6
    privately-run cells for drunks **254**.15
    smoking ban **261**.29
    and work **223**.23
    and young people **223**.28-9
    see also detention; youth custody
privacy **245**.1-39
    history of **245**.2-4
    Human Rights Act **196**.38; **245**.1
    and the law **245**.1-10
    and the media **210**.28, 33-9
        Human Rights Act **229**.5
    online **232**.28; **245**.3, 16-27; **266**.7, 18
    and social networking **210**.33-4; **230**.33-4; **266**.18
    see also freedom of information; personal
information
Privacy and Electronic Communications Regulations
    245.9
private life, right to **245**.1
private medical insurance **251**.5-6
    patients using NHS **251**.7
Privy Council **240**.22
pro-abortion (pro-choice) arguments **231**.1, 16
pro-eating disorder websites **249**.29-31
pro-life arguments **231**.1, 16
problem drinking see alcohol abuse
problem gambling **203**.2, 6, 19-39
    causes **203**.19
    children **203**.12, 15
    definition **203**.6, 12, 19
    genetic link **203**.30-31
    help **203**.21, 24-5, 34, 36
    Internet gambling **203**.28-9, 35-6
    people at risk **203**.23
    prevalence **203**.20
    signs **203**.2, 23
    social context **203**.32-3
    treatment **203**.24-5, 27
    women **203**.26, 35-6
    young people **203**.9-10, 11, 12, 15, 16
problem-solving therapy **265**.26
Proceeds of Crime Act and sex workers **246**.23
progestogen only pill (mini pill) **237**.6-7
Project HE:RO (Health Engagement: Real
Outcomes) **241**.35
prolonged grief **267**.3-4, 6-7
pronuclear transfer method, three-parent IVF **247**.29, 31
property crime **223**.4
proportional representation systems **240**.29
proscribed organizations **212**.15-16, 19
    Islamic **212**.10
prostitution **246**.17-29
    advice for sex workers **246**.21-3
    deterrents **246**.24-5

effects on society **246**.19-20
government policies **246**.17-18
and the law **246**.17, 18-19, 21-3, 28
legalisation debate **246**.20, 26
men's attitudes to **246**.24-5
reasons for using **246**.25
and sex trafficking **229**.19-20; **246**.29, 33
statistics **246**.19
Protect IP Act (PIPA) **230**.35-6, 37
Protecting the Public white paper **248**.1
Protection for Harassment Act and workplace stress **206**.29
Protection of Animals Act 1911 **233**.1-2
Protection of Children Act **248**.35
    and film classification **196**.14
Protection of Freedoms Act and CCTV **245**.32
proteins **214**.34
    dietary recommendations **271**.24
    and mental health **252**.25
    and vegetarian diet **214**.12, 29, 30, 33
Provincial Reconstruction Team, Afghanistan **259**.33
provocative victims of bullying **232**.8
Przewalski's horse **233**.26
PSHE (Personal, Social, Health and Economic) education
    covering sexualisation and gender stereotyping
        238.4, 11, 14
psychodynamic therapy **265**.26
psychological abuse as domestic abuse **224**.3
psychological effects
    of cannabis **256**.11-12, 20, 34, 35-6
    of human cloning **211**.27
    of sports injuries **270**.37-8
psychology of social media **266**.6-7
psychosis **201**.18-19
    and cannabis use **256**.12
psychotherapy and depression **265**.4
PTSD see post-traumatic stress disorder)
puberty and anorexia **249**.2, 17
pubic lice (crabs) **237**.21
public access to crime data **223**.1-2
public appointments, women **221**.14, 15
public attitudes
    to assisted suicide **217**.23, 34
    to biodiversity **216**.11; **218**.17
    to biotechnology **211**.5-6
    to burqa wearing **215**.39
    to business **227**.11, 13-14
    to cannabis decriminalisation and legalisation **256**.38
    to CCTV **245**.28, 29
    to climate change **216**.21, 24, 25, 32
    to Communications Data Bill **245**.8
    to disabled people **255**.10-11, 25-8, 37
    to environmental issues **218**.14
    to film classification **196**.15-16
    to food from cloned animals **211**.6, 11, 12, 14
    to genetically modified food **208**.18, 29-30; **211**.5
    on health care and the NHS **251**.19-22
    to homeless people **262**.12, 14-15, 16, 17
    to homeopathy **269**.32-3
    to human rights **229**.11-12
    to immigration **220**.22-3, 26, 27-8
    to inter-faith relations **212**.30-31
    to LGBT people **225**.11-13
    to mental ill health **201**.23
    to population growth **220**.10

to press self-regulation **196**.6
to same sex marriage **244**.22, 24-5, 27, 28, 29
to social mobility and earnings **219**.15
terrorism fears following London bombings **212**.4
to use of torture **229**.12, 22
Public Health England **251**.25, 31
Public Health Funerals **267**.35
Public Health Responsibility Deal **271**.6, 13-14
public interest and media regulation **210**.28
Public Order Act and film classification **196**.14
public sector cuts **227**.16
public sector employment, graduates **264**.34
public sector fraud **207**.21, 22
public services
    open data policies **245**.12-13
    and population growth **220**.7
Public Space Protection Orders (PSPOs) **262**.18
public transport
    and bicycles **200**.21
    city strategies **200**.30-31
    and disabled people **255**.17
    effects of London bombings **212**.4
    high prices **200**.16
    as terrorism targets **212**.7
    usage **200**.3
    see also buses; railways
pubs, role in the community **254**.39
punishment *see* penalties; sentencing
pupils
    assaults on staff **209**.16
    attitudes to learning styles **209**.1-3
    attitudes to school **209**.11
    behaviour and teacher stress **209**.15
Puppet on a String report (Barnardo's) **246**.35-6
Purdy, Debbie **217**.24
Putting Patients First **251**.4

Q

qualifications
    academic and vocational **209**.1-3
    see also A-levels; degrees; educational
achievement; GCSEs
quality time, parents **257**.25
Queen Elizabeth II **240**.22-3
quitting smoking *see* smoking, giving up
Quorn **214**.9
    and vegan diet **214**.29

R

Race Online 2012 **230**.21
Race Relations Act **236**.1-3, 16, 21
'race to the bottom', banana industry **226**.35
racial discrimination **236**.1-39
    definitions **236**.1-3
    and drug laws **228**.34
    against Gypsies and Travellers **236**.21-2
    see also racism

racial equality, global public attitudes **229**.12
racial harassment **236**.2-3
racism **236**.3-16, 21-39
    admission of racist feelings **236**.33
    casual racism **236**.29-30
    against East Europeans **236**.32
    experiences of **236**.6-12, 25
    in football **236**.9, 12, 13, 15, 25, 38; **270**.15
    indirect racism **236**.28
    and mental problems in young people **201**.2
    against Muslims *see* Islamophobia
    perceptions of **236**.3-5
    in the police **236**.26-7
    in schools **236**.15, 16
    on Twitter **232**.38; **236**.31
    violence **236**.13-15
    see also discrimination; employment and racism;
ethnic minorities; racial discrimination
racist bullying **232**.10, 11, 17; **236**.16
radicalism at universities **212**.13-14
radio
    broadcasting regulations **210**.27
    digital **210**.15
    and sexually explicit song lyrics **238**.20
    UK services **210**.3
RAF, and Strategic Defence and Security Review
    213.19
railways
    high-speed rail **200**.35, 36, 37-9
    light rail **200**.30, 33-4
    prices **200**.16
    suicide prevention measures **258**.32-3
    usage statistics **200**.3
Rainbow SPARX **265**.37
rainforests *see* forests
Ramsar Convention **260**.27
rape
    definition **237**.12
    myths about **237**.14
    reporting **237**.13-14
    and sexual imagery **238**.12
rapid-cycling bipolar disorder **201**.15
Rastafarianism and vegetarianism **214**.6
Razgour, Dr Orly **260**.7
Real IRA (RIRA) **212**.14
reality TV **210**.9
    and body image **234**.7
reasonable adjustments for disabled people **255**.15
    education providers **255**.29-30
    workplace **255**.29
recession
    and abortion rate **231**.13
    and gender pay gap **221**.23
    impact on immigration **220**.31
    impact on sport participation **270**.2
    and students' plans **209**.31
recombinant DNA technologies *see* genetic
modification
recovery programmes for offenders **223**.23-4
recruitment age, Armed Services **213**.15-16
recruitment of employees
    and age discrimination **239**.12-13
    disability rights **255**.29

and race discrimination **236**.20

use of social media **227**.38

recycling **218**.11; **242**.22-4, 33

and China's ban on plastic waste **242**.19

fines **242**.30

government policies **242**.3, 4

incentives **242**.31

increase in **242**.6

organic waste *see* composting waste

statistics **218**.12

red hair as cause of bullying **232**.16

Red List of Threatened Species **260**.1, 5, 22

Red Tractor assurance scheme **233**.3

REDD (Reducing Emissions from Deforestation in Developing Countries) **218**.20-21

reduce, reuse, recycle **218**.11

reducing waste **218**.11

see also recycling

referendum on Scottish independence **240**.32

reflexology **269**.2-3

refugees **235**.27; **259**.18-23

due to climate change **216**.10-11

legal definition **259**.23

refugee camps, Syria **259**.20

young, homelessness **262**.24

see also asylum seekers

refuges **220**.36-7

environmental **220**.39

for male victims of domestic abuse **224**.11

for teenage victims of relationship abuse **224**.19

refusal to engage (indirect racism) **236**.28

regeneration effect of tourism **222**.4

regenerative medicine

attitudes to **211**.6

see also embryonic stem cell research; stem cell research

registering a death **267**.28

regional and local government **240**.21, 27

regional nationalism **240**.8

Regulate, Control and Tax Cannabis Act, California **256**.31

regulation

animal experiments **233**.28, 33

assisted suicide **217**.8

broadcasters **196**.18-21

complementary and alternative medicine **269**.8-9, 16

films **196**.13-16

health care **251**.25-6, 31-2

herbal medicine **269**.13-14, 15

homeopathy **269**.12

Internet **196**.31, 36-7; **246**.7-8, 15-16

media **210**.27-9, 34

obscene publications 22-3

press **196**.6

private landlords **253**.12-13

see also legislation

Regulation of Investigative Powers Act (RIPA) **245**.32

Rehabilitation of Offenders Act **223**.27

relationships

breakdown, and homelessness **262**.24

and depression **265**.2, 3

effect of child abuse **248**.4

effect of pornography **246**.1, 11

ending

civil partnerships **244**.30-31

see also divorce; separation

and happiness **265**.38

and money worries **250**.33

and stress **206**.18

see also marriage

relative poverty **235**.2-3

relaxation

and anxiety **206**.12

effect of nicotine **261**.5

and mental health **252**.25-6

and stress **206**.34, 35

Release campaign for decriminalisation of drugs possession **228**.34

relief, humanitarian **259**.29-30

mobile apps for aid workers **266**.34

religion **215**.1-39

and abortion **231**.19, 39

attitudes to **212**.30-31I **215**.7-8

in Britain **215**.5-6, 8, 14, 15-16

and discrimination **215**.23-5; **225**.34, 35

effects of **215**.7-8

and euthanasia **217**.2, 4, 6

faith schools *see* faith schools

and the law **215**.26-7

media coverage **215**.13

as natural human inclination **215**.16

and pornography **246**.1

religious observance in Britain **215**.5-6 ,8, 14, 15-16

religious belief

and attitudes to death **267**.23

and same sex marriage **244**.19, 23, 25, 29

and support after bereavement **267**.3

and sport participation **270**.2, 24-5

statistics **215**.5-6

surveys **215**.5-6, 7-8, 15-16

in USA **215**.6

and vegetarianism **214**. 5, 6, 13

and war and peace **259**.3-5

see also churches; individual religions

religious discrimination at work **215**.23-4

religious education and faith schools **209**.23

religious freedom, global public attitudes **229**.12

religious marriage ceremonies **244**.2, 4, 8, 9

civil partnerships **244**.17

same sex couples **244**.19

religious offence **196**.11-12

religious organizations hosting civil partnerships **225**.32

religious slaughter **233**.16

religious tolerance **215**.23-39

and Islam **212**.32

religiously motivated crime

anti-Muslim hate crime **215**.28-30

remarriage **244**.3

remembrance of the deceased **267**.13-14

Facebook memorials **267**.15

roadside memorials **267**.16-17

see also funerals

remote gambling *see* online gambling

remote working **227**.2-3

renewable energy **204**.1, 2-8, 11-22, 25-7, 32; **218**.10

biofuels **204**.3, 26, 32, 34, 39

hydro power **204**.19, 27

microgeneration **204**.35-6

policies
   EU **204**.30-31
   UK **204**.7-8, 28-9
subsidies **204**.4
wave energy **204**.20, 26
see also energy efficiency; solar energy; wind energy
rented accommodation **253**.1, 10
   need for regulation **253**.11, **253**.12-13
   scams warning for students **264**.18
reoffending rates
   children **223**.31
   and employment **223**.26
reparative therapy, homosexuality **225**.2
repeat abortions **231**.11-12
reporting of suicide and self-harm, guidelines **258**.1
reporters, female **210**.7
reproductive cloning **211**.22, 24-7
   see also human reproductive cloning
reproductive ethics **247**.22-39
reproductive immunology **247**.8
reputation, online **266**.7, 18
research cloning **211**.32
resource consumption **218**.7-8, 13-14
   and population growth **220**.11-12, 14, 15
   water **218**.33
Respect Yourself website **237**.37
respiratory health and smoking **261**.1, 8
   see also lung cancer
Responsibility Deal **271**.6, 13-14
Responsibility to Protect **259**.27-8, 30-31
responsible travel **222**.35
   definition **222**.25
   see also ecotourism
restorative justice **223**.28-9
retail industry
   alcohol retailers' Code of Practice **254**.22
   crowdsourcing of CCTV monitoring **245**.30
   and environmentalism **207**.34
   and gender stereotyping **238**.34
   independent sector **207**.28
   and *Let Girls Be Girls* campaign **238**.9
   and sexualized products for children **238**.2-3, 5-6, 9, 31
   and shopper surveillance **245**.34-5
   statistics **207**.1
retargeting **230**.5
retirement **239**.14
   phased **263**.33
   saving for **250**.33, 36
   working after retirement age **239**.16, 18
   see also pensions
reusing goods **218**.11
Reuters, social media guidelines **210**.32
rewilding **260**.34-5, 36-7, 39
rhinoceros poaching **260**.9-11
rice, GM **208**.19, 29, 35
rich-poor gap **263**.12
   global **226**.17-18
   UK **235**.12, 13
right to die *see* assisted suicide; euthanasia
right to remain **259**.19
rights
   in abortion **231**.17, 18

children's *see* children's rights
consumer *see* consumer rights
to family life **245**.1
and the Internet **230**.30, 37, 38-9
to privacy **196**.38; **245**.1
sexual **196**.36, 38
at work **263**.4-5
see also human rights
Rights of the Child, UN Convention *see* under United Nations
riots of 2011
   and CCTV **245**.29
   children's sentences **223**.29
   reasons for **223**.8
   young people's reactions **223**.9-11
RIPA (Regulation of Investigative Powers Act) **245**.32
RIRA (Real IRA) **212**.14
risk behaviour
   international trends **252**.9-10
   and staying out late without parents knowing **252**.11-12
   see also alcohol abuse; drug abuse
Ritalin **252**.33, 34
road accidents **200**.12
   see also drink-driving
road charging **200**.9, 10
   congestion charging **200**.17-18
   public attitudes **200**.6
road tax (Vehicle Excise Duty) **200**.7
road traffic
   pollution *see* pollution and transport
   see also cars
Roadmap for European CAM Research **269**.10
roads
   arguments against building new roads **200**.7-8
   economic effects of new roads **200**.8
   funding **200**.6, 7, 9-10
   road surface material made from plastic bags **242**.28
   shared by cars and bikes **200**.18
   see also road charging
Robin Hood tax **235**.13-15
robotic weapons **259**.12
Roman Catholics *see* Catholic Church
romance and marriage **244**.4
Romanian migrants as victims of rasism **236**.32
Rome Statute of the International Criminal Court **259**.28
Ronaldo, Cristiano **270**.10-11
rough sleeping **262**.6, 9
   London **262**.32, 36
   support services **262**.36-7, 38
   see also homelessness
Rowntree, Seebohm **219**.11
Roy, Satyajit **261**.15
Royal Air Force and Strategic Defence and Security Review **213**.19
Royal Family **240**.23
Royal Navy and Strategic Defence and Security Review **213**.18-19
RSPCA (Royal Society for the Prevention of Cruelty to Animals) **233**.1
RtoP (Responsibility to Protect) **259**.27-8, 30-31
rubbish *see* waste
rumination syndrome **249**.8

runaway children and sexual exploitation **262**.28
running **241**.31, 32
    ability to run 100m **241**.13
    Zombies, Run! fitness app **241**.38-9
Russia
    child labour **268**.11
    privacy rights **245**.4

S

SAD (Seasonal Affective Disorder) **265**.2, 11
Saddam Hussein, UK selling weapons to **259**.11
safe houses *see* refuges
Safe Routes to Schools (SRS) projects **200**.2
safe sex **237**.1-2
    see also contraception
Safeguarding in Sport **270**.28-9
Safer Sex in the Adult Film Industry Act **246**.5
safety
    children **248**.9-11
    and cycling **200**.21
    e-cigarettes **261**.11, 13
    food from cloned animals **211**.18, 19
    of genetically modified food **208**.1, 2, 24
    human cloning **211**.26, 27
    and the Human Rights Act **229**.3
    at university **264**.17
safety and the Internet **232**.26-7; **230**.22-9
    children's safety **238**.5, 15, 26; **248**.10-11, 12
    identity fraud **230**.24, 30
    network filters **238**.16, 25, 26
    parental concerns **266**.19
    parental controls **238**.5
    personal privacy *see* privacy, online
    Safetynet petition **238**.26
    social networking **230**.23-4
    see also cyberbullying
salaries
    graduates **263**.25
    see also earnings; wages
salmon
    genetically modified **208**.31, 39
    as natural remedy **269**.27
Salmon Report on the NHS **251**.2
salt intake
    cutting down **271**.24
    health effects **271**.12
    Victorian diet **271**.2
Samaritans **258**.5
    guidelines on talking about suicide **258**.28
    helping prevent railway suicides **258**.32, 33
same-sex relationships
    and adoption **225**.34; **257**.17-18
    civil partnerships **244**.16-18
        in religious buildings **225**.32; **244**.17
    and domestic abuse **224**.5, 12-13
    human rights **229**.31-2
    and IVF treatment **247**.27
    marriage **225**.33; **244**.19-29
    medieval Europe **244**.5
    same-sex parents **257**.14-15
        represented in primary school books **257**.16

and surrogacy **247**.18-19
sanctions, countering weapons proliferation **259**.10
sanitation in developing countries **218**.31-3, 36
Sarah's Law **248**.35
SARC (sexual assault referral centre) **237**.14
SAT aptitude tests **219**.32
saturated fats **271**.15
    cutting down **271**.24
    food industry reduction pledge **271**.13-14
Saudi Arabia, death penalty **229**.37
savings
    children **250**.39
    families **257**.25
    lack of **250**.4, 26
    for old age **239**.14; **250**.33, 36
    young people **250**.26, 27-8
saviour siblings **211**.32; **247**.37-8
SAWS (Seasonal Agricultural Workers Scheme) **263**.10
Say Yes to 21ˢᵗ Century Sex and Relationships Education campaign **237**.36
schizophrenia **201**.16-17
    and cannabis use **228**.8; **256**.11-12, 34, 35-6
scholarships, students **250**.24
school bullying **232**.1, 5-6, 17
    dealing with bullying **232**.4, 18
    racist bullying **232**.10, 11, 17
    staff experiencing cyberbullying **232**.33, 34-6
school leaver programmes **264**.2, 6
school meals **252**.30-31
    and children's health **241**.20, 21
    School Food Standards **271**.34
    World Food Programme **229**.28
school nurses **252**.15
School Standard and Framework Act 1998 **225**.7
school uniforms and gender equality **268**.16
schools **209**.1-26
    academies **209**.25, 26
    admission systems **219**.24
    assaults on staff **209**.16
    and body image **234**.11, 21, 29-30
    bullying *see* school bullying
    carbon footprint reduction **200**.19-20
    and CCTV **245**.36-7
    and childhood obesity **241**.20
    and children in poverty **235**.22
    and children with same-sex parents **257**.15
    children's attitudes to **209**.1-3, 11
    citizenship education **240**.1-2, 38
    collecting data on children **245**.16
    controlled self-harm policy **258**.19
    curriculum reform **209**.5
    developing countries **229**.27-8
    and disabled children, Uganda **255**.39
    and disability rights **255**.29-30
    and ending violence against women and girls **224**.29
    employers' involvement **219**.26
    enterprise education **263**.28-9
    ex-service personnel as mentors **213**.32
    faith-based **209**.22-3, 24; **215**.17-22
    and financial education **250**.17, 19
    free schools **209**.19-21
        faith-based **215**.21-2
    and genderstereotype awareness **238**.14
    girl's non-attendance **221**.38-9

and healthy eating **271**.6, 34
    Tesco food education programme **271**.35-6
HPV (cervical cancer) vaccination **237**.31
ICT education **230**.13
journeys to **200**.1-2, 19-20
knife crime education **223**.16-17
and LGBT-inclusive materials **257**.17
and LGBT people **225**.5-8
online privacy education **245**.26
parent satisfaction **209**.21
parental presuure **209**.4
performance data publication **245**.12
and physical activity **241**.9; **271**.6
PSHE education, sexualisation and gender
stereotyping **238**.4, 11, 14
and racism **236**.15, 16
same-sex marriage education **244**.21, 24
school system reform **209**.6
school type and pupil's degree perfomance **219**.32
selective, and social mobility **219**.31
self-harm policy at specialist school **258**.19
sex education *see* sex education
single-sex **221**.30-32
and social mobility **219**.18, 23, 28, 31
and social networking skills **266**.25-6
and special educational needs **255**.30
sports
    funding **270**.38-9
    girls' reluctance to participate **270**.23
    LGBT inclusivity **270**.17
    visits by cricketers **270**.7
standards **209**.7-10
suicide discussion **258**.28
travel plans **200**.2
and violent extremism **212**.12
Youth Parliament manifesto **240**.38
see also education; National Curriculum;
secondary schools; teachers
SCNT *see* somatic-cell nuclear transfer
Scotland
abortion law **231**.3
crime statistics **223**.2
drug strategy **228**.24
empty homes **253**.33
euthanasia legislation rejection **217**. 30
feelings of Scottish identity **240**.8, 12, 18
free school meals **271**.37
gangs and knife crime **223**.6-7
Gypsy Travellers **236**.22
health and physical activity **241**.1-4
homophobic crime **225**.30
independence **240**.5, 6, 32
palliative care **217**.18
parliament **240**.27
physical activity levels **241**.1
smoking **261**.36-7
smoking ban **261**.32
statutory housing provision **262**.3
scratch and sniff cards to help detect cannabis
farms **256**.39
sea level rise **216**.9, 16-17, 20-21
effect on island nations **220**.38
seal hunting **233**.22-3

seas *see* marine environments
Seasonal Affective Disorder (SAD) **265**.2, 11
Seasonal Agricultural Workers Scheme (SAWS) **263**.10
SeaWorld, slavery case **233**.21
second-hand smoke *see* passive smoking
secondary infertility **247**.4
secondary schools
    see A-levels; GCSEs; schools
Secretary of State for Health **251**.30
secularism
as argument for banning burqa **215**.36
in Britain **215**.15
security
as reason for banning burqa **215**.35
and social networking **210**.30-31
at university **264**.17
seed hybridization **211**.2
selective eating **249**.23-4
selective schools and social mobility **219**.31
Selective Serotonin Re-uptake Inhibitors (SSRIs) **265**.20
selenium
in red meat **214**.34-5
and vegetarian diets **214**.29
self-affirmation **234**.3
Self Assessment tax returns **250**.13
self-blame *see* blame, feelings of
self-defence and protection against bullying **232**.21
self-directed violence *see* self-harm; suicide
self-employment and National Insurance **250**.15
self-esteem
Dove campaign **234**.33
and child abuse **248**.4
and eating disorders **249**.3
impact of pornography **246**.1
and sport **270**.5-6
see also body image
self-exclusion and depression **265**.7
self-harm **252**.22-3; **258**.1-19
avoidance techniques **258**.4, 12, 13-14
behaviour **258**.2, 8, 10, 18
and bullying **232**.9
causes **258**.2, 10, 17
controlled self-harm policy in school **258**.19
definition **258**.2
following child abuse **248**.5
getting help **258**.3, 5, 12, 13-14
long-term risks **258**.3-4, 7
prevalence **258**.2, 8, 10
reasons **258**.7, 8-9, 10, 18
risk factors **258**.17
risk groups **258**.2
self-help **258**.3, 4-5, 12, 13-14
signs **258**.7, 17-18
and social media **266**.6, 9-10, 11, 12
and suicide **258**.7, 8
support groups **258**.3
treatment **258**.3, 5, 14, 15
self help
for alcohol dependence **254**.9
for anxiety problems **206**.12
books, depression **265**.31
for depression **252**.19; **265**.2, 22, 31
for eating disorders **249**.3-4

improving mental health **252**.25-6
    for self-harming behaviour **258**.3, 4-5, 12, 13-14
    for stress **206**.3-4, 27
    for suicidal thoughts **258**.26-7
self-image *see* body image
self-regulation of the press **196**.6
self-stigma
    HIV sufferers **243**.17
    mental illness **201**.28
SEN (Special Educational Needs) **255**.30
sensible drinking **254**.7, 11-12, 17, 35-6
sentencing **223**.19-20, 21
    children **223**.29, 30
    community sentences **223**.20, 23
    for drugs offences **228**.23, 28-31
    and maturity of young offenders **223**.33-4
    terrorism offences **212**.9-10, 19
separation
    couples unable to afford to separate **244**.38-9
    effect on children **244**.36-7; **257**.12, 13
    online help **244**.34
    see also divorce; parental separation
serious games (preparation for work) **263**.23
serotonin and mental health **201**.33
serotonin-adrenaline reuptake inhibitors (SNRIs) **265**.20
servitude, definition **268**.39
sex
    attitudes to, and pornography **246**.1, 2-3
    effects of smoking **261**.8
sex discrimination
    in the Army **213**.13-14
    see also gender inequality
sex education **238**.4, 14-15; **237**.15-16, 33-9
    failure of **237**.33, 35-6
    and LBGT relationships **225**.7
    in schools **237**.15-16, 35-6
    and unplanned pregnancies **237**.8
    website **237**.37
sex offences, statistics **223**.5
sex offenders
    and IVF treatment **247**.27
    registration, and Human Rights Act **229**.6
Sex Offenders Act 1997 **248**.35
sex-selection
    abortion **231**.18, 30-31
    of embryos **247**.35, 36
sex stereotyping *see* gender stereotyping
sex trafficking **229**.17; **246**.23, 25, 30-32
    of boys and men **246**.39
    of children **246**.35-6, 37; **268**.31
    definition **246**.30
    and prostitution **229**.19-20; **246**.29, 33
sex workers
    advice for **246**.21-3
    and HIV **243**.6
    see also prostitution
sexting **221**.9-10; **230**.26-7; **238**.23-4; **246**.11
sexual abuse **248**.3, 5-7, 26-31
    among children **238**.17; **248**.13
    of children, in sports **270**.26-7
    and children's mental health problems **201**.3
    definition **248**.5, 26
    as domestic abuse **224**.1, 3
    effects **248**.26

getting help **248**.26-7
perpetrators **248**.6, 26
prevalence **248**.5-6
support for victims in court **248**.39
among young people **238**.15
sexual abusers *see* sex offenders
sexual assault
    definition **237**.12
    reporting **237**.13-14
    see also rape
sexual behaviour, teenagers **237**.15-17
sexual bullying **221**.11
sexual consent and the law **237**.12-14
sexual content on the Internet **196**.36-9
    child abuse **196**.39
sexual exploitation of children **268**.31, 32-4, 35-6
    perpetrators **268**.33-4
    runaway children **262**.28
    signs and symptoms **268**.32-3
    victims **268**.34, 35-6
    see also child pornography; child prostitution
sexual function, effects of alcohol **254**.3
sexual health **237**.1-17
    and alcohol **254**.6
    safe sex **237**.1-2
    see also contraception; sex education; sexually
transmitted infections
sexual offences, statistics **223**.5
Sexual Offences Act **246**.17, 18; **248**.1, 35
sexual orientation **225**.1-18
    altering **225**.2, 16, 17-18
    attitudes to **225**.11-13
    and bullying *see* homophobic bullying
    causes **225**.1-2, 15-16
    definitions **225**.3, 5, 19-20
    discovering **225**.1
    discrimination **225**.9-10, 28-9, 35
    and the law **225**.28-39
    and sport participation **270**.1-2, 16-19
    and teenage homelessness **262**.15
    and US military **225**.38-9
    see also gay men; lesbians; LGBT people;
transgender people
sexual rights **196**.36
    threats to **196**.38
sexual transmission of HIV **243**.1
sexualisation **238**.1-39; **246**.12, 13
    Bailey Review **238**.2, 5-7, 8, 33, 34
    of children **238**.1-37, 38-9
    children's clothing and products **238**.1, 5-6, 8-9,
        10, 13, 31, 32-3, 36
    definition **238**.1
    effect of the media **196**.25-6; 3, 13, 32-3
    effects on children **238**.2, 8, 9
    of women **221**.34; **238**.37-8
    of boys **238**.1, 3
    of young girls **221**.9-10; **238**.1, 3, 8-9, 13, 27-33
        parents' complicity **238**.36-7
sexuality *see* sexual orientation
sexually transmitted infections (STIs) **237**.1-2, 18-25
    chlamydia **237**.20, 22, 24; **252**.2, 3
    and fertility **247**.5
    genital warts **237**.20

gonorrhoea **237**.20-21, 24-5
hepatitis B **237**.21
herpes **237**.20
infection rates **237**.10, 24-5
knowledge about **237**.23
protection against **237**.1-2, 4, 18-19
pubic lice (crabs) **237**.21
symptoms **237**.4, 19, 20-21, 22
syphilis **237**.21
testing for **237**.22, 24
gay and bisexual men **243**.9
and young people **237**.24-5; **252**.2, 3
see also AIDS; HIV
shared ownership home-buying schemes **253**.8
Sharia law **215**.11-12
shipping containers as accommodation for
homeless people **262**.31
shisha **261**.2, 3, 10
shoes, leather and vegetarianism **214**.13
shopping
addiction to **207**.6
Internet see Internet shopping
shopper surveillance **245**.34-5
see also consumer rights; consumerism;
consumers; retail industry
shops, empty **207**.9
Shulman, Alexandra **234**.5-6
Siberian (Amur) tigers **260**.1
siblings
effect on teenage pregnancy **257**.33
saviour **211**.32; **247**.37-8
Sideline Bad Behaviour campaign **270**.28-9
sight problems with ageing **239**.4, 25-6
Sikhism **215**.3
and abortion **231**.19
and pornography **246**.1
and vegetarianism **214**.6
and war and peace **259**.4
single income families **257**.29
single parent families
and child maintenance **257**.30-31
UK **257**.11-12
worldwide **257**.3-4
single people and homelessness **262**.1-2, 3
single-sex education
boys **221**.30
girls **221**.31-2
Single Transferable Vote **240**.29
skills gap, young people **263**.21
skin, effects of alcohol **254**.6
skunk (cannabis) **256**.1, 12-13
slavery in the UK **268**.39
sleep
advice for students **264**.24
and mental health, teenagers **201**.7
young people **252**.4, 27, 28
Sleep Out homelessness awareness campaign **262**.37
sleep-related eating disorder **249**.8
sleeping rough see rough sleeping
slums **235**.36-8
slum tourism **222**.16, 33-4
slutwalk protests **221**.12
small businesses

costs of fraud **207**.22
difficulties **227**.8
start-ups **227**.5
statistics **227**.6
smart drugs **252**.33, 34
smart working **263**.18
smartphones **210**.11, 13-14
booking travel **222**.9
children viewing inappropriate content **238**.19
and shopper surveillance **245**.34
Smedley, Peter (assisted suicide) **217**.20
smoking **261**.1-39
alcohol **254**.33-4
cannabis see cannabis
children **252**.37-9; **261**.6, 20, 38-9
costs of **261**.9, 21, 26
e-cigarettes **261**.11-12, 13, 25, 37
effects on appearance **261**.8-9, 25
effects on fertility **247**.3, 5
in films **261**.18-19
giving up **261**.5, 10, 17, 21, 26
and health **261**.1, 2-3, 4, 8-9, 10
benefits of giving up **261**.9, 17, 21
history of **261**.3
Indonesia **261**.38-9
passive smoking **261**.1, 14, 28-9
reasons for **261**.4-5
Scotland **261**.36-7
smoking bans **261**.31-2
in cars with child passengers **261**.28-9
and reduction in premature births **261**.32
in prisons **261**.29
social smoking **261**.17
and stress **206**.33
third-hand smoke **261**.15
trends **261**.6-7
young people **252**.1-2, 31, 35, 37-8
social activity, older people **239**.27, 38, 39
social bookmarking services **266**.1-2
social care
care crisis for disabled people **255**.23-4
economic benefits **255**.36
older people see care services for older people
social capital and health **219**.12
social class
and health **219**.11-13
middle classes **219**.1-2, 9-10
working classes **219**.3-4, 5-6
and educational attainment **219**.29-30
see also social mobility
social drinking, young people **254**.30
social exclusion **235**.2
and sexual orientation **225**.9-10
social factors
and gambling **203**.32-3
and malnutrition **271**.4
and obesity **271**.8
Social Fund Funeral Payment scheme **267**.34-5
social gambling **203**.12
social housing **253**.13-14
lifetime tenancies **253**.15
and immigrants **220**.28, 29
social inequality

and child labour **268**.4

and children, UK **268**.18

social isolation *see* loneliness

social media *see* social networking

social mobility **219**.14-39

and education **219**.18, 22, 23, 25-6, 27-8, 34-5

government strategy **219**.17-21

perceptions of **219**.15

prejudice against **219**.4

rate of **219**.14

Social Mobility and Child Poverty Commission **219**.19

social networking **210**.5, 12, 14; **252**.9; **266**.1-39

addiction **266**.13

birth parents contacting adopted children **247**.16

and bullying **232**.25, 26-7, 28; **258**.36-7; **265**.18

and business ethics **227**.37-9

and charity sector **266**.35-7

and children **266**.19, 20, 22-3

and advertising **266**.24

teaching skills in school **266**.25-6

closing a deceased's account **267**.38

and data mining **245**.23-4

and depression **265**.18

eating disorder promotion **249**.29, 30

forms of **266**.1-2

friendships **265**.18

and gambling **203**.17

and gender **230**.2, 3

history of **266**.2-4

and older people **266**.16

parents monitoring children's use **245**.26-7

positive uses **266**.27-39

and privacy **210**.33-4; **230**.33-4; 18, 25-6

and psychology **266**.6-7

and racism **236**.31

and relationship abuse **224**.16-17

reporting inappropriate content **232**.35

safety **230**.23-4

security issues **210**.30-31

and self-esteem **266**.6, 9-10, 11, 12

and teenage suicide prevention **258**.38-9

and travel **222**.9

underage use **266**.22-3

worldwide usage **266**.5, 8

and young people **266**.17, 18

see also Facebook

social security benefits *see* state benefits

social smoking **261**.17

social welfare

history **219**.11

see also state benefits

social welfare law problems and mental health, young people **201**.29-30

societies, university **264**.22-3, 28-9

socio-economic groups

and academic performance **209**.13-14

and cannabis use **256**.16

and higher education participation **209**.34-5

and smoking **261**.6-7

see also social class

soft drinks, sugar content **271**.19

solar energy

solar electricity **204**.3, 25, 35–6

from space **204**.39

subsidies **204**.7

water heating **204**.3, 21-2, 25, 35

soldiers

child *see* child soldiers

suicides **258**.31

soliciting **246**.23

solvent and volatile substance abuse **228**.7, 15

SOPA (Stop Online Piracy Act) **230**.35-6, 37

Sorting Out Separation web app **244**.34

South Africa

as gap year destination **222**.19

privacy rights **245**.4

wellbeing of older people **239**.9

sovereign debt **226**.5

space, solar energy collection **204**.39

space rationing (housing policy) **253**.17

space tourism **222**.17-18

Spain, smoking ban **261**.32

SPARX (computerized CBT for depression) **265**.36-7

SPCA (Society for the Prevention to Cruelty to Animals) **233**.1

Special Educational Needs (SEN) **255**.30

Special Representative of the Secretary-General for Children and Armed Conflict **268**.26

species conservation, zoos **233**.25, 26

species loss **220**.6; **260**.2-3, 4-5

spending

and budgeting **250**.37-8

on communications **210**.12

on holidays **222**.5, 6-7

household **207**.7, 8

personal **207**.6

sperm production and fertility **247**.2, 3

Spirit of Cricket school assemblies **270**.7

spiritual brotherhoods **244**.5

sponsored degree programmes **264**.1, 3

sponsorship and advertising to children **207**.39

sport **270**.1-39

betting **203**.8

and bullying **232**.1-2, 7

and child abuse **270**.26-28

for children **241**.35-6

and disabled people **255**.14-15; **270**.12-14

and drugs *see* drugs in sport

and ethnic minorities **236**.12

hijab ban in professional basketball **270**.24-5

injuries **270**.36-8

legacy of Olympic Games **241**.9, 10

and LGBT people **270**.16-19

match fixing **270**.33

media coverage of women's sport **270**.20-22

participation **270**.1-2, 3

and racism **236**.9, 12, 13, 15, 25, 38, 39

poverty gap **241**.29-30

school sports funding **270**.38-9

and self-esteem **270**.5-6

sexualized promotion of sportswomen **238**.37-8

sports events and sex trafficking **229**.20

success attributes of top athletes **270**.10-11

working conditions of professional sports players **270**. 8-9

and young people **270**.4-6

see also football; Olympic Games; Paralympic Games

Sportivate **270**.1
Sportsister **270**.21-2
SportWatch **270**.20-21
spread betting **203**.4
Spurs football club, 'anti-Semitic' chants **236**.39
squatting **262**.13, 25
SSRIs (Selective Serotonin Re-Uptake Inhibitors) **265**.20
St John's wort **252**.19
    depression treatment **265**.3, 25
stakeholder theory of corporate social responsibility **227**.10
stalking **224**.5
start-ups, business **227**.5
state benefits **263**.6-9
    benefit fraud **219**.5-6; **263**.6-7
    disabled people
        benefit cuts **229**.32; **255**.34, 35, 38
        benefit scrounger rhetoric **255**.10-11, 37
    and food poverty **271**.3
    help with funeral costs **267**.34-5
    and National Insurance **250**.15-16
    reforms **263**.9
    rented housing discrimination against claimants **253**.12
    and welfare reform bill **235**.9
    welfare spending and economic performance **263**.8
    see also disability benefits
stations, suicide prevention measures **258**.32-3
status dogs **233**.4
statutory homelessness **262**.3
staycations **222**.5
staying out late without parents knowing **252**.11-12
stem cell research **211**.29-37
    embryonic **211**.29-32
    ethical issues **211**.30-31, 34
    induced pluripotent stem cells **211**.35-7
stem cell therapy **211**.30
    for multiple sclerosis **211**.38-9
stem cell transplants, saviour siblings **211**.32; **247**.37-8
stem cells **211**.28, 29-30
    embryonic **211**.28, 29-30, 35-6
    from aborted fetuses **211**.33
    iPS **211**.35-7
    tissue-specific (adult) **211**.28, 29
stepfamilies **257**.21-3
stereotyping
    age **239**.4-5, 6
    gender *see* gender stereotyping
    racial **236**.34
steroids **228**.26; **270**.30-31
STIs *see* sexually transmitted infections
stiff upper lip (British reserve) **267**.4-5
stigma
    of depression **265**.6-7
    of disabled children **255**.25-8
    of living with HIV **243**.15-17
    of self-harm **258**.9
    of teenage parents **257**.32-3
stillbirth **267**.21-2
stimulants (uppers) **228**.3
    signs of use **228**.14
    and sports, risks **270**.31-2
    see also ecstasy

stoke (surfing) **265**.30-31
stomach, effects of alcohol **254**.3, 5
stop and search
    anti-Muslim discrimination **212**.28-9
    Terrorism Act **212**.16
Stop Online Piracy Act (SOPA) **230**.35-6, 37
Stop Smoking Service (NHS) **261**.10, 24
stopping smoking **261**.5, 10, 17, 21, 26
    health benefits **261**.9, 17, 21
Stoptober challenge **261**.26
stranger danger **248**.9-10
Strategic Defence and Security Review **213**.17-19
    criticism of **213**.20-21
street design for sustainable transport **200**.30
street sleeping *see* rough sleeping
Street View (Google) and privacy **210**.33; **245**.38-9
StreetLink **262**.36-7, 38
stress
    causes **206**.17-31
    complications **206**.4
    coping with **206**.32-9
    and exams **252**.16-17
    self help **206**.3-4, 27
    signs and symptoms **206**.1-2, 7-9, 17, 19
    statistics on **206**.5, 21
    students **206**.38-9; **264**.30
    treatment **206**.2-4
    work-related *see* work-related stress
    young people **252**.4, 5-6
strip clubs **246**.23
strokes **239**.26; **241**.3-4
    stem cell therapy **211**.33
students
    accommodation **209**.30
    binge drinking **252**.36
    black students, employment prospects **236**.19-20
    dropping out **209**.32
    eating disorders **249**.15
    homesickness **264**.16
    lifestyle **209**.30-33
    LGBT, and sport **270**.16-17
    and money matters **209**.31-2
        budgeting **264**.19
        debt **264**.20, 29
        financial help **206**.39
        grants and loans **250**.22-5
    safety on nights out **254**.35-6
    satisfaction surveys **264**.26, 27
    and security **264**.17
    and sleep **264**.24
    social media and student engagement **266**.30-31
    and stress **206**.38-9
    student life **264**.14-31
Students Union **209**.30
submissive victims of bullying **232**.8
subsidies
    definition **226**.30
    impact on developing countries **226**.33
substance abuse *see* alcohol abuse; drug abuse; solvent abuse
suction aspiration (abortion) **231**.7
sugar **271**.16-22
    cutting down **271**.24

health effects **271**.18-19, 21
and mental health **252**.25
sugar reduction campaign **271**.20
types **271**.16-17
Sugar Puffs, complaints about marketing to children **271**.30
suicidal feelings **258**.26-7, 34, 35
and antidepressants **265**.21-2
and bullying **232**.9
how to help someone **258**.23-4, 25
young people **258**.38-9
suicide **258**.20-39
and alcohol consumption **254**.6
and bullying **232**.9
copycat suicides **258**.26
and cyberbullying **258**.36-7
media reporting guidelines **258**.1
prevention **258**.20, 22-4
railway stations **258**.32-3
using social media and mobile phones **258**.
38-9
risk factors **258**.20, 24
and self-harm **258**.3, 7, 8
statistics **252**.1; **258**.20, 21, 33
suicide terrorism
condemned by Islam **215**.10-11
Great Britain **212**.5-6
use of children **212**.11-12
in teenage fiction **258**.30
warning signs **258**.22, 24
young people **252**.1; 24, 36-7, 38-9; **267**.20
see also assisted suicide; physician-assisted
suicide (PAS)
Suicide Act and assisted suicide **217**.24
Sumatra, destruction of tiger habitat **260**.12
super-farms **233**.3, 9-11
super-fast broadband **210**.15
supermarkets
and meat free products **214**.7
threat to local shops **207**.26, 27
vegetarian food availability **214**.9
Supplementary Vote (SV) **240**.29
support groups
alcohol dependence **254**.9
gamblers **203**.25
stress and anxiety sufferers **206**.3, 12; **252**.14-15
Supporting People (homelessness support) **262**.8-9
surfing, mental health benefits **265**.30-31
surgery
restriction for smokers and obese people **261**.22-3
risks to smokers **261**.9
weight loss *see* bariatric surgery
surgical abortion **231**.7
surrogacy **247**.18-19
health risks, surrogate mothers in India **247**.20-21
surveillance **245**.28-39
CCTV **245**.28-32, 36-7
by the government **245**.32
by the retail sector **245**.34-5
in schools **245**.36-7
suspended prison sentences **223**.19
sustainability
cities **218**.6
eco-towns **253**.36
fisheries **218**.23

and marine environments **218**.22
and population growth **218**.5
and resource use **218**.7-8
sustainable agriculture **214**.14, 20-21
sustainable development **226**.3-4
sustainable housing **253**.37
sustainable tourism **222**.8-9, 21-3
definition **222**.25
see also ecotourism; responsible travel
sustainable transport networks **200**.30-31
swearing on television **196**.21
Sweden
free schools **209**.20
health care **251**.9
housework gender division **263**.15
importing waste for waste-to-energy plants **242**.37
LGBT equality policy **225**.13
modeling agencies targeting eating disorder
sufferers **249**.26
sex education **237**.34
smoking ban **261**.32
sweeteners **271**.11
Switzerland, assisted suicide **217**.2
Swizzles, complaints about marketing to children
271.30
symmetrical families **257**.6-7
synthetic cannabinoids **256**.3-4
syphilis **237**.21
Syria
displaced persons **259**.20, 21
reasons for military intervention **259**.35-6

T

Takhi (Przewalski's horse) **233**.26
TalkTalk, Internet filter service **238**.16, 25
talking
about death **267**.24-5, 27
Death Cafes **267**.11
about self-harm feelings **258**.12, 13
about suicide **258**.22-3, 25
with school pupils **258**.28
to a suicidal person **258**.22-4, 25
see also communication
talking therapies **252**.19
and depression **265**.4, 22, 24, 26
see also cognitive behavioural therapy;
counselling
Tanzania, education improvements **229**.27
tariffs **226**.13, 26-7
taxation
air travel **222**.14-15
alcohol
and beer industry **254**.39
and young people's drinking **254**.21
and cannabis market **256**.10
Council Tax **250**.14
ending 50p rate **219**.7
as ethical investment issue **227**.33
family impacts of tax and benefit changes **257**.
26-7
on financial sector **235**.13-15

high earners opinions of **227**.25
Income Tax **250**.13
and multination corporations **227**.32-3
National Insurance **250**.15
and NHS funding **251**.20-21
and road building **200**.7
tax havens **227**.34-6
and trade **226**.13, 26-7
on unhealthy food **241**.20-21
VAT **250**.14
TB *see* tuberculosis
TCAs (tricyclic antidepressants) **265**.20
teachers
assaults by pupils **209**.16
attitudes to school learning styles **209**.1-3
and cyberbullying **232**.33, 34-6
faith schools **209**.23
influence on children's attainment **219**.33
racist bullying **236**.16
and same sex marriage education **244**.21, 24
stress caused by pupil behaviour **209**.15
Team Dignitas (video gaming) **270**.35
technology use
business trends **227**.1-3
Middle Britain **219**.2
supporting care for older people **239**.38
teenage fiction and suicide **258**.30
teenage parents **257**.32-9
a mother's story **257**.35-6
support for fathers **257**.34
teenage pregnancies
sibling effect **257**.33
statistics **257**.32
unplanned **237**.8, 10
teenage relationship abuse **224**.4, 16-21, 35-6
teenage suicide
and cyberbullying **258**.36-7
prevention and intervention initiatives **258**.38-9
teenagers *see* young people
teeth and human diet **214**.12
teetotalers, young people **254**.26
telecommunications
broadband services **210**.15; **230**.6-8
international comparisons **210**.13-15
prices, international comparisons **210**.14-15
statistics **210**.10
trends **210**.4-5, 10-16
telephones, mobile *see* mobile phones
television
and body image **234**.7, 19
junk food advertising **271**.27-8
offensive language **196**.21, 24
pre-watershed programming **238**.5
reality television *see* reality television
regulation **196**.18-20; **210**.27
sexual content of programmes for young people **238**.13-14
UK services **210**.3
viewing habits **210**.4, 11
telomeres and ageing **239**.1
temperature of the earth
changes **216**.8, 9
measurement **216**.26-7
see also climate change; global warming

temporary accommodation **262**.6, 11
temporary class drug orders **228**.25
tenants, protection **253**.11, 12-13
TENS machines and dementia treatment **269**.22
terminally ill people *see* assisted suicide;
euthanasia; hospices; palliative care
termination *see* abortion
terraced housing **253**.31
Territorial Army (TA) **213**.30
terrorism **212**.1-39
and Communications Data Bill **245**.5
counter-terrorism **212**.15-25
legislation **212**.15-16, 19, 20
police powers **212**.15-16
review **212**.21-2, 26, 38-9
definition **212**.1, 15
effects **212**.2-3
and Islam **212**.32
Islamist **212**.8-10
London bombings **212**.4, 5
reasons for **212**.1
suicide terrorism
Great Britain **212**.5-6
use of children **212**.11-12
Terrorism Acts **212**.15-16, 19
Terrorism Prevention and Investigation Measures
Bill **212**.20
in the UK **212**.5-7, 8-10
effect on the public **212**.4
by Irish Republican groups **212**.14
by Islamists **212**.8-10
Terry, John **236**.38
Tesco
food education programme **271**.35-6
virtual store **245**.35
test tube babies *see* in vitro fertilisation
tetrahydrocannabinol *see* THC
text messaging
and bullying **232**.17, 29
and suicide prevention initiatives **258**.38-9
Thailand as gap year destination **222**.19
therapy, family *see* family therapy
thermohaline circulation **216**.8
Thinspo (Thinspiration) **249**.29, 30
thiomersal and autism **255**.7
third-hand smoke **261**.15
Third World *see* developing countries
threats as domestic abuse **224**.1
three-parent IVF **247**.29-34
tidal power **204**.26
tigers
impact of habitat destruction **260**.12
poaching **260**.13-15; **269**.17
Siberian, endangered status **260**.1
tiger tourism **222**.26
Time on Our Side **263**.35
time limit for abortion **231**.21-3
time management, and stress **206**.18, 34, 35
TNCs *see* transnational corporations
tobacco **261**.2-3
chewing **261**.10
Victorians' use **271**.2
see also cigarettes; smoking; tobacco products

tobacco industry
    child labour **261**.9, 39
    and e-cigarettes **261**.12
    environmental costs **261**.9
    worker health **261**.9
Tobacco Product Directive **261**.27, 34
tobacco products
    in films **261**.18-19
    gateway effects of e-cigarettes **261**.12, 13
    marketing, impact on children **261**.33, 39
    purchase age, New York **261**.30
    see also cigarettes
toll roads **200**.9, 10
Too Good to Waste campaign **242**.39
top jobs, gender gap **221**.13-22
tortoise, giant, and forest restoration **260**.39
torture
    public attitudes to **229**.12, 22
    UK complicity in **229**.21-3
    by US soldiers **212**.36-7
Tottenham Hotspurs, 'anti-Semitic' chants **236**.39
tourism
    alternative **222**.16, 24
    Britain as holiday destination **222**.2-3, 5, 11
    and climate change **216**.12
    destination choice **222**.2-3, 11
    economic benefits **222**.4-5, 28, 30
    and endangered species **222**.26
    environmental impact **222**.21, 22, 25, 27, 28, 29
    and ethics **222**.31-2
    gap year destinations **222**.19
    holiday spending **222**.5, 6-7
    and London Olympics **222**.12-13
    slum tourism **222**.16, 33-4
    space tourism **222**.17-18
    sustainable tourism **222**.8-9, 21-3, 25
    trends **222**.1-3, 8-9
    volunteer tourism **222**.8, 27-8, 36-9
    see also ecotourism; holidays; responsible
tourism
toxic chemicals in tobacco smoke **261**.3
toxicity
    emissions from waste incineration **242**.35-6
    and GM crops **208**.27
    nanotechnology **208**.16
toys, colour coding and gender **221**.7-8
trade
    definition **226**.26
    illegal trade in wildlife **260**.16-26
    in indecent articles **196**.23
    international *see* international trade
    in ivory **260**.17, 20
      and poaching **260**.9-11, 24-5
trade footprint **226**.34
trade justice **226**.29, 33
trade liberalisation *see* free trade
trade negotiations and WTO agreements **226**.8
trade rules **226**.27
    see also World Trade Organization
Traditional Herbal Medicines Products Directive
(THMPD) **269**.13, 15
traditional medicine **269**.7
    see also herbal medicines
traffic *see* road traffic

traffic pollution *see* pollution and transport
trafficking **229**.17-20
    and child labour **268**.11
    children, UK **268**.36-7
    definition **268**.39
    and illegal adoption **268**.38-9
    see also sex trafficking
Trafficking in Persons (TIP) report **268**.38
train stations, suicide prevention measures **258**.32-3
training, vocational, and gender **221**.28
trains *see* railways
trams **200**.29, 33, 34
tranquilizers and phobia treatment **206**.13
trans (hydrogenated) fat **271**.15
transaction sex **268**.35
Transatlantic Trends survey **220**.22-3
transgender people **225**.5, 19-27
    definitions **225**.19-20
    and domestic abuse **224**.5, 12-13
    experiences **225**.21-2
    hate crime against **225**.30-31
    and marriage **225**.27
    and competitive sport **270**.18-19
transgenic technology *see* genetic modification
Transition to Adulthood (T2A) Alliance **223**.33
transnational corporations (TNCs) **226**.1, 27
transphobia **225**.7-8
transport **200**.1-39
    electric vehicles **200**.26-9
    emissions *see* emissions
    and the environment **200**.14-39
    and global poverty **200**.13
    and inequality **218**.3, 4
    noise **200**.14-15, 22
    policies **200**.15
    and schools **200**.1-2, 19-20
    sustainable transport networks **200**.30-31
    trends **200**.1-13
    see also air travel; cars; public transport; railways
transracial adoption **247**.16
transsexual people
    definition **225**.19
    and marriage **225**.27; **244**.1
    public figures **225**.25-6
transvestites **225**.19
trapping animals for fur **233**.18
trauma as cause of anxiety **206**.11
travel *see* air travel; transport; tourism
travel agents **222**.3
travel behaviour **222**.3
travel health advice **222**.10
travel information sources, new technologies **222**.9
Travellers and racial discrimination **236**.21-2
treatment
    alcohol dependence **254**.9
    anxiety problems **206**.12; **252**.15
    bipolar disorder **201**.15
    dementia **239**.29
    depression **239**.31; **252**.19; **265**.11, 12-13, 17, 19-37
    drug abuse effects **228**.2
    drug dependency **228**.16-18
    eating disorders **249**.32-9
    HIV **243**.3-4, 6, 32-5, 37-9

of homosexuality **225**.2, 16, 17-18
obesity **241**.18, 22
  see also weight management
panic attacks **206**.16
phobias **206**.12-13
psychosis **201**.18-19
Seasonal Affective Disorder **265**.11
self-harm injuries **258**.5
self-harm behaviour **258**.3, 14, 15
stress **206**.2-4
see also self help
trees
  adaptation to megafauna **260**.34
  diseases, UK **260**.22
  as memorials **267**.13
  see also forests
Trekstock **240**.35
triad of impairments, autistic spectrum disorders **255**.7
tricyclic antidepressants (TCAs) **265**.20
Trojan gene effect **208**.39
trolling **232**.32, 37
  how to handle trolls **266**.15
  sadistic nature of trolls **266**.14
trophic cascades **260**.6, 36
tuberculosis
  and HIV sufferers
    global incidence **243**.6, 27
    UK incidence **243**.5
  and homeless people **262**.33
turmeric as natural remedy **269**.27
tuition fees, university
  loans **250**.23
  as reason for not applying **264**.12
Turkey, domestic violence **224**.32-3
Tusk Trust **260**.8, 9
Twitter **210**.18
  criticism of Communications Data Bill **245**.6
  and narcissism **266**.9
  and racist abuse **232**.38; **236**.31

U

UDAW (Universal Declaration on Animal Welfare) **233**.2
Uganda
  aid and disabled people **255**.39
  GM bananas **208**.1
  withdrawal of aid due to anti-gay laws **225**.14
Ugly Mugs scheme for sex worker protection **246**.18, 19
UK **240**.3, 21-2
  and Afghanistan operations **259**.32-3
  AIDS strategy support **243**.28
  arms sales **259**.11
  and children's rights **229**.24, 29-30; **268**.17-19
  climate change impacts **216**.9
  climate change targets **216**.33
  conservation project investment **260**.28-9
  counter-terrorism strategy **212**.17-18
    review **212**.21-2, 38-9
  economy **227**.3

endangered species **260**.1, 21
energy policy **204**.7-8, 28-9
genetically modified crops **208**.5, 17-18, 25-6
government and politics **240**.21-2, 25-31
herbal medicine regulation **269**.14
hidden children **268**.36-7
HIV/AIDS statistics **243**.2, 5, 14-15
immigration **220**.20-21, 24-5
nuclear weapons **259**.15
population diversity **240**.15-16
population goals **220**.19
poverty **235**.1-22
terrorism **212**.4, 5-7, 8-10, 14
tiger protection programme support **269**.17
and torture complicity **229**.21-3
tourism **222**.1-3, 4-5, 11
trade initiatives **226**.28
wildlife review of 2013 **260**.21-2
Youth Parliament **240**.38-9
see also entries under British
UN *see* United Nations
unborn babies, effects of domestic abuse **224**.24, 37
UNCLOS (Convention on the Law of the Sea) **260**.27-8
unconventional therapies **269**.7
  see also complementary and alternative medicine
underage gambling **203**.12-14
underage use of social networking sites **266**.22-3
undergraduates *see* students
undernutrition **271**.5
underoccupation
  and housing benefit cuts **235**.9
  and housing redistribution **253**.17
unemployment **235**.6; **263**.1-3
  benefits **263**.7, 9
  black graduates **236**.19-20
  ethnic minorities **236**.10-11
  graduates and non-graduates **264**.33
  measuring **263**.2
  older people with HIV **243**.31
  as reason for return migration **220**.34
  statistics **227**.16; **263**.3
  trends **263**.1-2
  young people **263**.19-20, 21-3
    and mental health **252**.21; **265**.15
UNESCO, education programmes **229**.28
unhappiness, children and young people **258**.29
UNICEF
  Child Trafficking report and illegal adoption **268**.38
  projects **229**.24-6
Unilever, advertising **234**.22-3
Union Flag **240**.4-5
United Nations (UN)
  body image event **234**.37
  business and human rights **227**.27, 28
  and children in armed conflict **268**.14, 24-5, 26
  climate change conferences **216**.37, 38, 39
  Convention on Disability Rights **255**.30
  Convention on the Law of the Sea (UNCLOS) **260**.27-8
  Convention on the Rights of the Child **229**.24-6, 29; **248**.35
    and child labour **268**.2

and children in armed conflict **268**.14, 24-5
  and justice for children suffering human rights
abuses **268**.15
  Economic and Social Commission for Western
Asia (ESCWA) **229**.28
    education programmes **229**.28
    encouraging vegan diet **214**.24
    and human rights of lesbian, gay, bisexual and
transgender people **229**.31-2
    humanitarian relief **259**.29-30
    military interventions **259**.30-31
    Palermo Protocol (prevention of trafficking) **229**.17
    peacekeeping operations **259**.37, 38
    Population Fund (UNFPA) **229**.28
      report on ageing population **239**.13
    public attitudes to UN role in human rights **229**.11
    REDD rainforest protection programme **218**.20-21
    sanctions **259**.10
    see also Millennium Development Goals
units of alcohol **254**.2, 11-12
  and physical and mental effects **254**.7
Universal Credit **263**.9
  impact on youth homelessness **262**.29
Universal Declaration of Human Rights **229**.1
  and business **227**.28
universities **209**.27-39
  application numbers **209**.37-8
  black students **236**.19-20
  business partnerships **264**.6
  climate change emails, University of East Anglia
    216.22
  clubs and societies **264**.22-3, 28-9
  compared with apprenticeships **264**.9
  costs and benefits **264**.11, 12
  and ethnic minorities **236**.10, 19-20
  and extremism **212**.13-14
  funding **209**.29, 31-2, 35
    Youth Parliament manifesto **240**.38
  and gender segregation **264**.21-2
  paid-for places **219**.30, 36
  predictor of degree results **219**.32
  pupil mentoring and applying to university **264**.5
  reasons for not going to university **209**.27, 28
    fees **264**.12
  and social class **209**.34-5
  social media use to improve student engagement
    266.30-31
  student finance **209**.31-2; **250**.22-5
  student life **209**.30-33; **264**.14-31
  top ten rankings **264**.29
  see also degrees; further education; higher
education; students
unmanned drones **259**.12, 13
unreasonable behaviour as grounds for divorce **244**.30, 31
unsaturated fat **271**.15
uppers *see* stimulants
urban areas
  mental health benefits of green spaces **265**.35
  and sustainability **218**.6
  sustainable transport networks **200**.30-31
urban extensions **253**.20
USA
  AIDS strategy support **243**.28
  armed forces and sexual orientation **225**.38-9

cannabis laws **256**.28-9
Charter Schools **209**.20
death penalty **223**.39; **229**.37
and euthanasia **217**.2, 11
IVF clinics offering sex selection **247**.36
online piracy laws **230**.35-6
privacy rights **245**.4
religious belief **215**.6
torture of prisoners by soldiers **212**.36-7

V

vaccines
  and autism **255**.7
  benefits of **233**.33
  against HPV (cervical cancer) **237**.26-7, 28, 29-31
  production from GM plants **208**.21-2
vandalism, racist **236**.14
vaping *see* e-cigarettes
vascular dementia **201**.10; **239**.28
VAT (Value Added Tax) **250**.14
veganism **214**.1, 2, 3
  and children **214**.28
  and health **214**.37
  and heart-related diseases **214**.33
  reasons for **214**.3; **233**.2
  United Nations encouragement of **214**.24
vegetables *see* fruit and vegetables
vegetarian diets **214**.1, 2
vegetarianism **214**.1-39
  and children **214**.28, 36
  definition **214**.1, 28
  and the environment **214**.15-27
  and health **214**.5, 12, 28-9, 31-2, 38-9
  history of **214**.4
  and religion **214**.5, 6, 13
  reasons for becoming vegetarian **214**.4-5, 13
  types of vegetarianism **214**.1, 2
Vehicle Excise Duty (car tax) **200**.7
veils, Muslim women **215**.34-9
vending machines, interactive **245**.34-5
vertical occupational segregation **221**.27
veterans *see* ex-service personnel
Veto Violence campaign **240**.35
victimisation **225**.28
  definition **221**.3
  of mental health sufferers **201**.22
  racial **236**.2
victims of bullying **232**.2, 8
  characteristics **232**.2, 8, 31
  effects of bullying **232**.3, 8, 21, 25, 26
  feelings **232**.21, 26
  what to do **232**.18, 26
victims of conflict
  children **259**.25-6
  increase in fatalities **259**.6
  refugees **259**.18-23
victims of crime
  mental health sufferers **201**.22
  and restorative justice **223**.29
  role in justice system **223**.24
victims of domestic abuse **224**.2

disabled people **224**.4
getting help **224**.38
LGBT people **224**.5, 12-13
male **224**.5, 9-10, 11
older people **224**.4
pregnant women **224**.4-5
reasons for not leaving **224**.6
young people **224**.4, 16-21, 24, 25
women **224**.2, 3-4, 11
Victorian era, diet **271**.1-2
video games
age ratings **196**.17
as competitive sport **270**.34-6
Video Recordings Act 1984 **196**.14
videocasting **266**.1
videos
cyberbullying **232**.29
and data protection **232**.35
see also films
vInspired **240**.35
violence
against children **268**.13
against girls **221**.37, 38
against Muslims **215**.28-30
against school staff **209**.16
by children **224**.22-3
and gangs **223**.6-7, 13-15
and mental ill health **201**.22, 26
as obscenity **196**.22
in pornography **246**.2
against women **221**.37
impact of sexual imagery **238**.10-12
men's attitudes **246**.25
see also domestic abuse; physical abuse; sexual
abuse
violent crime, trends **223**.4
violent extremism
condemned by Islam **215**.10
in schools **212**.12
in universities **212**.13-14
VIPER (Voice, Inclusion, Participation,
Empowerment and Research) **255**.12-13
Virgin Media, criticims of Communications Data Bill **245**.6
virtual offices **227**.2-3
virtual stores **245**.35
virtual travel **266**.32-3
Virtual World platforms **266**.1
vision impairment with ageing **239**.4, 26-7
vitamins
in meat **214**.34
supplements **214**.10, 29
and vegetarian diet **214**.28, 29, 30, 33
vitamin D **214**.34
vivisection *see* animal experimentation
vocational colleges **264**.7
vocational qualifications
attitudes to **209**.1-3
see also specialist diplomas
vocational training and gender **221**.28
vodcasts **266**.1
Vogue magazine **234**.5-6
voice, children's rights to **229**.25-6
Voice over Internet Protocol (VoIP) **210**.13

void marriages **244**.3
volatile substance abuse *see* solvent abuse
voluntary activity **240**.33-6
Big Society **240**.33-4
by disabled people **270**.13
gap year volunteering **240**.36
older people **239**.27
rights and expenses **264**.38
volunteer tourism **222**.8, 27-8, 36-9
young people **240**.33-4, 35-6
voluntary euthanasia *see* assisted suicide
vomiting, eating disorders **249**.2
voting
lowering voting age **240**.30-31, 39
prisoners' right to vote **229**.35-6
voting systems **240**.29
women's right to vote **221**.36
Voxer app **266**.34
vulnerable employment, developing countries **235**.26
vulnerable people and assisted dying legalization
217.7-8, 12, 19, 32, 33, 39

W

W-curve and first year of university **264**.14-15
wages
ethnic pay gap **236**.18
garment industry **229**.13
high earners' attitudes to **227**.24-5
inequality **227**.15, 16
minimum wage **263**.5-6
public perceptions of wage levels **219**.15
soldiers **213**.1
see also earnings; incomes; salaries
waist measurement and health risk **241**.14-15
Wales
abortion law **231**.3
drug strategy **228**.24
empty homes **253**.32
feelings of Welsh identity **240**.8, 12, 18
health and physical activity **241**.1-4
National Assembly **240**.27
opt-out organ donation **267**.39
plastic bag charge **242**.25
priority need for housing **262**.3
smoking ban **261**.32
sports schemes to close poverty gap **241**.29-30
walking
and mental health **252**.26
to school **200**.7
see also exercise
Wallace, Bethaney **234**.36
Wan, Gok **234**.19
war and conflict **259**.1-39
as cause of migration **220**.36-7; **259**.18-21, 22
and children **259**.25-6
consequences of war **259**.18-26
justification for military intervention **259**.29, 35-6
laws of war **259**.1, 7-8

and religious teachings **259**.3-5
trends in armed conflicts **259**.6, 36-7
and women's rights in Afghanistan and Iraq **259**.34
see also Armed Forces; child soldiers; weapons
war crimes **259**.8, 28
and child soldiers **259**.24
Warsi, Baroness Sayeeda **215**.31-2
waste **218**.11-12; **242**.1-39
electronic **218**.15-16; **242**.20-21
EU exports **242**.19
and energy generation **204**.6, 24; **242**.32-3
export of waste **242**.18-19, 22
illegal **242**.10, 11-12
from Norway to Sweden **242**.37
food **242**.3, 14-16, 38-9; **271**.2
government policies **242**.1-4, 9
hazardous **218**.12
EU trade **242**.18-19
illegal dumping **242**.10-11
illegal activities **242**.8-9, 10-12
incineration **242**.34-6
plant threatening waste pickers' jobs **242**.29
producing energy **242**.32-3
Sweden importing waste for energy plants **242**.37
landfill **242**.5, 7
litter **242**.13, 17
plastic bags **242**.25-7, 28
reducing waste **218**.11
see also household waste; landfill; litter; organic waste;
recycling
Waste-as-Resource(WaR) facilities **242**.33
waste bins, homeless people dying in **262**.21
Waste from Electrical and Electronic Equipment (WEEE) **242**.20-21
waste hierarchy **218**.11; **242**.2
water consumption
in diet **271**.7, 31
reducing **218**.34-5
statistics **218**.36-7
water pipes (tobacco smoking) **261**.2, 3, 10
water pollution **218**.38-9
water power **204**.19, 27
water supplies
and agriculture **214**.17
and climate change **216**.6, 10
drinking water access, developing countries **218**.31-3, 36
and GM crops **208**.20
and population growth **220**.6
scarcity **218**.33
water voles **260**.21
watershed
for music videos and lyrics **238**.20
television **238**.5, 20
wave energy **204**.20, 26
Wave Project **265**.30-31
wealth
inherited **219**.8
inequalities *see* rich-poor gap
weapons
arms trade **259**.11, 16-17
countering weapons proliferation **259**.10

gun crime **223**.5
knife crime *see* knife crime
landmines **259**.9, 39
nuclear **259**.14-15
robotic **259**.12
weather
events of 2010 **216**.5, 13
predictions, UK **216**.9
websites
blocking **196**.38
newspapers **210**.19
promoting eating disorders **249**.29-31
WEEE (Waste from Electrical and Electronic Equipment) **242**.20-21
weight *see* body weight; obesity
weight loss
and Quorn **214**.9
surgery **241**.18, 22
weight problems *see* obesity; underweight people
welfare reform bill **235**.9, 10
welfare support *see* state benefits
West Antarctic ice sheet **216**.12
Western countries *see* developed countries
whales
animal rights **233**.20, 21
whale watching holidays **222**.26
whistleblowing on athletes using drugs **270**.32
white British pupils, poverty and academic performance **209**.13-14; **219**.29-30
Whitehouse, Mary **196**.25-6
WHO *see* World Health Organisation
WikiLeaks **210**.20-26
wikis **266**.1
wild animals in circuses **233**.4, 14-15
wildlife
conservation **260**.27-39
review of 2013 **260**.21-2
tourism **222**.26
trade, illegal **260**.16-26
see also conservation; endangered species; extinction
William, Duke of Cambridge, on endangered animals **260**.8-9
wills **267**.29, 30
living *see* advance directives
wind farms **204**.13-18
costs **204**.17-18
impacts on local communities **204**.12
offshore **204**.14-18
under-performance **204**.13, 18
wind power **204**.3, 11-18, 25-6; **218**.10
EU targets **204**.11
microgeneration **204**.35
UK targets **204**.8, 17
Windsor and Maidenhead, rewards for recycling **242**.31
Winehouse, Amy
death prompting call for drugs education **228**.10-11
suffering from bulimia **249**.24
winter fuel payments **204**.23
witchcraft accusations and child abuse **248**.21-3
withdrawal symptoms
cannabis **256**.12

gambling **203**.6
withdrawing medical treatment **217**.14
wolves, Yellowstone National Park **260**.37
women
    and abortion **231**.18-19
      right to choose **231**.17, 25
    Afghanistan, effect of war **259**.34
    and Armed Forces **213**.12-14
    body image concerns **234**.14-15
    career aspirations **221**.21
    as domestic abuse perpetrators **224**.9-10
    as domestic abuse victims **224**.2, 3-4, 11
    eating disorders **249**.12, 15-16
    and exercise **241**.11-12
    and fertility *see* fertility
    and gambling
      online gambling **203**.35-6
      as target of gaming companies **203**.26
    gender pay gap **221**.22-5, 27-8, 35-6, 37
    glass ceiling **221**.21-2
    and HIV/AIDS **243**.6
      diagnosis during pregnancy **243**.13
      transmission to baby **243**.1-2, 25
    and homelessness **262**.2
    and household tasks **221**.6; **263**.15
    and inequality **221**.1-2, 33-6, 37
    Internet usage **230**.2-3
    Iraq, effect of war **259**.34
    IVF procedure **247**.9-10, 11-12
    marriage expectations **244**.6-7
    media usage **210**.12
    migrant workers **220**.35
    Muslim
      ban on hijab in basketball **270**.24-5
      and face veils **215**.34-9
      as victims of hate crime **215**.29
    and the news **210**.6-8
    older women and IVF **247**.10, 22-6
    and politics **221**.2, 13, 15, 20, 36, 37
    and pornography industry **246**.3, 4-5
    effects of prostitution **246**.19-20, 27-8
    and provocative clothing **221**.12
    rights
      Afghanistan and Iraq, following wars **259**.34
      global public attitudes **229**.12
    sexualisation, compliance in **238**.36-8
    and sexually transmitted infections (STIs) **237**.4, 19, 22
    shopaholism **207**.6
    sport
      barriers to participation **270**.22
      media coverage **270**.20-22
      impact of school PE **270**.23
    and stress **206**.8-9
    voting rights **221**.36
    working hours and divorce **244**.33
    see also girls and young women; mothers;
pregnancy; working mothers
women in the workforce
    boardroom positions **221**.14, 15, 16, 17-18, 21-2, 37
    equal pay *see* gender pay gap
    glass ceiling **221**.21-2

    in senior positions **221**.13-22
    see also working mothers
Women Chainmakers of Cradley Heath **221**.35
wood fuelled heating **204**.36
wood waste trade, EU **242**.18
work
    effects of cannabis use **256**.11
    and childcare costs **257**.29
    effect of money worries **250**.33
    flexible working **263**.17-18, 33-4
    and gender *see* gender and work
    and homeless people **262**.14-15; 39
      selling the Big Issue **262**.17
    in prison **223**.23
    past retirement age **239**.16, 18
    unequal distribution of work **263**.39
    workers' rights **229**.14-16; **263**.4-5
    working patterns **263**.17-18, 33-9
    young people **263**.19-30
    see also child labour; employment; housework;
  migrant workers; older workers; unemployment
work-based learning programmes **264**.6
work-bound people and digital travel **266**.32-3
Work Capability Assessment **263**.9
Work Choice **255**.31
work experience
    increasing chance of getting graduate job
      263.24, 25; **264**.28
    internships **264**.36-7
work-family balance **257**.24
work-life balance **263**.31-9
    see also hours of work
Work Programme **255**.31
work-related stress **206**.7-9, 17-18, 24-9; **263**.31, 36
    causes **206**.29; **263**.31
    costs **206**.5
    legislation **206**.25, 28-9
    signs **206**.7-9
working age dementia **201**.10-11
working class, prejudice against **219**.3-6
working conditions
    developing countries
      garment industry, campaign for living wage
        229.13
      improvement initiatives **226**.28
    professional sports players **270**.8-9
working hours **263**.35, 37-8
    long working hours and stress on parents **206**. 22-3
working mothers, effects on children **221**.26
working parents and stress **206**.22-3
workless household **263**.6, 13-14
workplace
    age discrimination **239**.6, 12-13
    and disability rights **255**.29
    drug misuse signs **228**.15
    gender balance **221**.19
      boardroom positions **221**.14, 15, 16, 17-18, 20, 21-2, 37
    new technology and working practices **227**.1-3
    sexual orientation discrimination **225**.9, 28-9
    stress *see* work-related stress

workplace bullying **232**.23, 24
    cyberbullying **227**.38
workplace pensions **250**.12
World Bank **226**.9-10
    and gender equality **221**.2
    and poverty reduction **235**.23-4, 32
World Food Programme, school meals provision
    229.28
World Health Organization
    mental health programmes **201**.8-9
world trade *see* international trade
World Trade Organization (WTO) **226**.1, 7-8, 14-15
    criticism of **226**.14-15, 32
    trade rules **226**.27
Wu, Venzen **265**.31

Y

yeast in Victorian diet **271**.1-2
Yellowstone National Park, reintroduction of wolves
    260.37
Yemen, death penalty **229**.37
Yizhi capsule and dementia treatment **269**.22
young carers **201**.8-9
    mental health problems **201**.4
    and neglect **248**.15
young children
    eating disorders **249**.3, 7-8, 22
    sexualisation of girls **221**.9-10
Young Life and Times survey (Northern Ireland)
    237.15-17
young offenders
    maturity as a factor in sentencing **223**.33-4
    and prison **223**.28-9
young onset dementia **201**.10-11
young people
    and age discrimination **239**.6
    in the Armed Forces **213**.15-16
    attitudes to ageing **239**.6-7
    attitudes to higher education **209**.27-8
    attitudes to riots **223**.9, 10-11
    and bariatric surgery **241**.22
    and body image **234**.7, 26
    and cannabis **256**.5-6
        mental health effects **256**.11-12
        penalties for possession **256**.2
        unaware of risks **256**.6, 21
    caring for parents with mental health problems **201**.
      8-9
    causes of death **267**.20
    and contraceptive information **237**.8-9
    and cosmetic surgery **234**.33, 34
    and crime *see* young offenders; youth crime
    and criminal justice system **223**.25
        maturity as a factor in sentencing **223**.33-4
    and cyberbullying **232**.30-32; **258**.36-7
    and depression **265**.15, 16-17, 18, 21-2
        computerized CBT treatment **265**.36-7
        digital fluency **230**.10-12
    disabled, decision-making participation **255**.

    12-13
    and domestic abuse **224**.16-26
        effects of domestic abuse **224**.24-5
        teenage relationship abuse **224**.4, 16-21, 35-6
    and drug abuse **228**.1; **252**.1, 31, 32, 35
        treatment **228**.17
    education on HIV/AIDS **243**.10-11
    entrepreneurship **227**.6; **264**.10-11
    financial skills **250**.17, 18
    and gambling **203**.9-18
        Internet gambling **203**.16-18
        problem gambling **203**.9-10, 12, 15, 16, 20
        reasons for gambling **203**.9
    gang membership **223**.6-7, 13-15
    girls in prostitution **246**.27-8, 34-8
    health **252**.1-12
        and happiness **241**.8
    and HIV/AIDS **243**.10-11, 23-5
    and home ownership **253**.2-3, 4
    homelessness **262**.15, 22-30
    HPV (cervical cancer) vaccination **237**.27, 28,
      29-31
    and identity fraud risk **245**.21-2
    and the Internet **230**.4-5, 8-13, 33-4
    and marriage **244**.1
    media usage **210**.5, 11
    and mental health **252**.13-26
    and mental health problems **201**.2-4, 29-30
    and mental health services **201**.36
    men using prostitutes **246**.24
    mentoring by ex-service personnel **213**.32
    and modelling **234**.35
    and money **250**.17-28
    not in employment, education or training (NEET)
      252.21
    online counseling service **258**.16
    parenthood *see* teenage parents
    physical activity guidelines **241**.6
    and pornography **238**.3-4; **246**.10-11, 12, 13
    and pregnancy *see* teenage pregnancies
    savings **250**.26, 27-8, 36
    and self-harm **252**.22-3; **258**.10, 17-18
    sexual behaviour **237**.15-17
    and sexual orientation **225**.1, 2-3, 5-8
    and sexually transmitted infections (STIs) **237**.10,
      23, 24-5; **252**.2, 3
    and sexual violence **238**.15
    sleep deprivation and mental health **201**.7
    and smoking **252**.1-2, 31, 35, 37-9
        influence of smoking in films **261**.18-19
    and social media **266**.17
    and social mobility **219**.18
    and sport
        effect of injuries **270**.37
        participation **270**.1, 4
        self-esteem and moral development **270**.5-6
    and suicide **258**.24, 36-7, 38-9
    unemployment **263**.19-20, 21-3
        and mental health problems **265**.15
    unhappiness **258**.29
    and vegetarian diet **214**.36
    and volunteering **240**.33-4, 35-6
    and work **263**.19-30
young people and alcohol

Vol. numbers appear first (in bold) followed by page numbers; a change in volume is preceded by a semi-colon. You can also find this title list at the front of the book.